Jan van Waarde

Acknowledgements/Credits
The author wishes to extend special thanks to John Bessette, a former member of the 7499th Support Squadron. John, who was also the 7499th Group Association Historian, provided invaluable help in creating this book. Other individuals who contributed are Stephen Miller, Henk Scharringa, Peter Zastrow, Frank Cooper, Manfred Faber, Herb Greathouse, Albert O'Connor II, Lindsay Peacock, and Dave Wilton.
Credits also go to the websites www.9websites.com/airforce and www.globalsecurity.com, and Doug Gordon's *Tactical Reconnaissance in the Cold War*. Furthermore, special thanks to the Air Force Historical Research Agency (AFHRA), Maxwell Air Force Base, Alabama.

Photo acknowledgment
Most photographs in this publication are from the United States Air Force (USAF) archives, the National Archives and Records Administration (NARA), and other public records. The photographs in this book are individually credited.

Every reasonable effort has been made to trace copyright holders and obtain their permission to use the photo material. The publisher apologizes for errors or omissions in this work and would be grateful if notified of any corrections that should be incorporated in future reprints or editions of this book.

Copyright © 2024 - All rights reserved.
No part of this book may be reproduced or transmitted in any form or by any means, electronic or mechanical, including photocopying, recording, or any information storage and retrieval system, without the publisher's permission in writing.

Book proposals
Aviation History Research & Publishing welcomes book proposals in fields appropriate for Aviation History's editorial program. Please see our website for more information about how to craft your proposal and what to include:
www.aviationhistory.nl/submission
Send your proposal to: editor@aviationhistory.nl

Secret Mission - COLD WAR spy flights in Europe

Contents

All-out intelligence	-	Page 9
Dancing the corridors	-	Page 22
The eavesdroppers	-	Page 36
Behind the curtain	-	Page 48
Index	-	Page 58

Martin RB-57D 53-3972 was with 4025th SRS/408oth SRW at Laughlin AFB; before it was modernised under the Dinah Lee program at the General Dynamics facility in Fort Worth. As single seat RB-57D-1 itswas delivered to 7407th SS at Rhein-Main on June 9, 1959. In 1964 it was shipped back to the USA and stored MASDC (Military Aircraft Storage and Disposition Center), Phoenix, Arizona. Later, the airframe was used for RB-57F. Photo: U.S. Air Force.

Secret Mission

In 1948, Wiesbaden Air Base, also known as Lindsey Air Station, located near the town of Wiesbaden on the River Rhine, served as a crucial hub supporting the Berlin Airlift Operation Vittles. It operated around-the-clock flights to Tempelhof Airport. Douglas C-47 Skytrains and Douglas C-54 Skymasters of the 60th Troop Carrier Group conducted daily missions to Tempelhof in the beleaguered city of Berlin. During this period, Wiesbaden also became a central base for the United States Air Force in Europe (USAFE), with its headquarters at Wiesbaden Air Base. The base facilitated numerous reconnaissance and spy flights using converted B-29 bombers, as well as C-54, C-118, and C-130 transport aircraft. These flights were conducted along the Eastern European borders and in the Berlin air corridors. Subsequently, dedicated reconnaissance jet planes, such as supersonic North American RF-100s from Bitburg Air Base, high-flying Lockheed U-2s, and, from nearby Rhein-Main Air Base, long-winged RB-57s, were employed.
These aircraft were deployed to peer and gather intelligence on Soviet military activities, radar stations, air bases, and naval bases. They collected both photographic and electronic information and were utilized in covert overflight programs. The 1952 photo captures nearly fifty aircraft of various types.
Photo: U.S. Air Force.

Secret Mission is a book about a little-known chapter in USAF history, but a very important one during the Cold War.
In the early 1980s, I was one of the aviation enthusiasts that frequented the observation spot at Soesterberg air base, watching (and photographing) the comings and goings of the based F-15 Eagles.

Occasionally, there were some interesting visitors, and in August 1984, a rather anonymous-looking C-130E shot a few approaches, and I learned that the aircraft was assigned to the 7405th Support Squadron from Rhein-Main.

This was when I first became aware of the existence of a unit that flew spy missions in the shadow of the regular C-130 transport fleet at Rhein-Main. Although the unit had a very innocent and non-descriptive designation, its mission was not!

This sparked a lifelong interest in the early reconnaissance missions over the Soviet Union and the Eastern-Bloc countries, at first with some rudimentary reconnaissance aircraft.

Later on, these were equipped with increasingly sophisticated reconnaissance suites. This was a very dangerous mission, with lots of hair-raising incidents, culminating in Gary Powers' U-2 downing over Sverdlovsk in 1960, which ended manned reconnaissance flights over Warszaw Pact territories. Apart from the Berlin mission, that is.

These reconnaissance operations continued until the Berlin Wall came down in November 1989. The history of this mission is recounted in this book, which would not have been possible without the invaluable help of John Bessette, the historian of the 7499th Group Association and a former member of the unit, who shared his stories and knowledge with me.

Jan van Waarde

During the Berlin airlift (Operation Vittles) and due to the growing tensions between East and West, the USAFE decided to form its reconnaissance and ELINT units into a single squadron. The 7499th Air Force Squadron was activated at Fürstenfeldbruck on November 1, 1948. For better management of this covert outfit and to bring it closer to the major USAFE photo and ELINT interpretation centres, the 7499th, in August 1950, moved to Wiesbaden Air Base, close to the USAFE Headquarters located in the same city. In 1955, in response to increasing collection requirements, USAFE upgraded its reconnaissance effort, creating the 7499th Support Group at Wiesbaden with three support squadrons: the 7405th, the 7406th, and the 7407th.

A gun camera photo from the Soviet MiG-17 shows the moment it shot down a U.S. Air Force reconnaissance-configured C-130 aircraft over Soviet Armenia, resulting in the tragic deaths of the seventeen crew members aboard. The attack occurred on September 2, 1958, after the unarmed aircraft inadvertently entered denied airspace. The C-130, with tail number 60528, was stationed at Rhein-Main Air Base in Germany but temporarily deployed to Incirlik Air Base, Adana, Turkey. The aircraft carried six crew members from the 7406th Support Squadron and eleven USAF specialists from Detachment One of the 6911th Radio Group Mobile, based in Darmstadt, Germany. Soviet involvement in the incident remained secret for thirty-three years until 1991 when the Soviets released detailed information to U.S. authorities, confirming the shooting down. The U.S. National Security Agency (NSA) declassified the documents in August 2009. See also pages 40-41. Photo: PVO.

Chapter One

All-out intelligence

The year is 1945. Hitler's Nazi Germany had almost been defeated. In February of that year, the Allied leaders, Stalin, Churchill, and Roosevelt, gathered at Yalta for a conference that would change the course of world history for the following 45 years.

During this conference, the leaders decided on the postwar situation in Europe and the Pacific. In Europe, countries in what was to become Western Europe would come under the influence of the USA and its Allies, while Eastern European countries would have to answer to the Soviet Union. Germany itself was to be divided into four occupation zones.

Following the Soviet blockade of Berlin in 1948, the Soviet zone became East Germany, while the three "Western" zones (controlled by the United States, Britain and France) became West Germany.

An Iron Curtain

The German capital city Berlin was divided in equal fashion. Austria, which declared independence from Germany in April 1945, was divided along the same lines, with Vienna being divided the same way Berlin was. However, in 1955, allied occupation of Austria ended and it was declared a neutral country. Once the division of Germany had taken effect, the Soviet Union firmly closed the borders with the West and effectively separated their territory with what Winston Churchill later described as "An Iron Curtain." Due to the ravages of war and the efforts to rebuild the European society, the Western powers had so far hardly made any effort in keeping their intelligence efforts in Eastern Europe up to date, and once the borders had been closed, they soon realized that the accuracy of the maps of those countries, for instance, was woefully inadequate,

Chapter One - All-out intelligence

Among the squadron's initial aircraft, RB-17G 44-8889 holds a prominent position. Serving with the 7499th CS from approximately 1948 to 1953, this aircraft specialized in gathering electronic intelligence (ELINT) data. Its missions spanned the East-West German border, the Berlin corridors, and over the Baltic and Adriatic Seas. Later, the aircraft found a new purpose when it was sold to the French Institut Géographique Nationale (IGN) and given the civil registration F-BGSO. Under the IGN's ownership, the aircraft underwent significant modifications tailored for survey work. It embarked on numerous photo-mapping missions worldwide, leaving an indelible mark on aerial endeavors. On September 8, 1976, the B-17 was generously donated to the Musée de l'Air in Le Bourget near Paris, France, where it is currently preserved in storage. Photo: Robert Brewer via 7499th Group Association.

and that there was no easy way to improve this shortcoming.

To remedy this, an all-out intelligence and reconnaissance effort was started, and high-flying Allied aircraft started flying "secret" reconnaissance missions around, and sometimes over, areas of the Eastern Bloc that were of interest to Allied military planners, like naval ports and air bases. Initially, a variety of aircraft types was used for these missions, like RAF Mosquitos and USAF Boeing RB-29s, which, due to their superior performance, could operate with relative impunity in the late 1940s.

Soviet counter actions

However, the Soviet Union intensified its efforts to counter these reconnaissance missions, resulting in several disastrous outcomes. Sixteen American aircraft engaged in reconnaissance missions were either shot down by the Soviets or lost in other ways, although most of these incidents occurred during peripheral missions. The most infamous among them was the destruction of Francis Gary Powers' Lockheed U-2 over Sverdlovsk in 1960. This incident marked the end of the early overflights. President Eisenhower displayed extreme reluctance, to say the least, in approving any new overflights, and officially, no further missions over Soviet territory were conducted, at least not by the USAF. However, their counterparts in Pakistan and National China did continue such missions with the assistance of the United States.

Along the borders of the Eastern Bloc

However, there were comparatively less risky strategic reconnaissance missions that could be carried out, specifically peripheral missions conducted along the borders of the Eastern Bloc. The air corridors leading from the West into Berlin and Vienna were of particular interest, with Allied planners finding the eastern part of Germany especially intriguing. From the late 1940s onward, the USAF dedicated substantial resources and funding to develop reconnaissance systems, resulting in the establishment of a substantial fleet of strategic reconnaissance aircraft. This fleet comprised numerous Boeing RB-47s,

RB-50s, Convair RB-36s, and eventually Boeing RC-135s, along with several other less prevalent aircraft types. The U.S. Navy also played a role, albeit on a smaller scale. It is worth noting that this book does not account for the significant number of tactical reconnaissance aircraft such as Lockheed RF-80As, Republic RF-84Fs, McDonnell RF-101s, and RF-4Cs, which were assigned distinct missions.

Mission shrouded in secrecy

During the late 1940s, airborne reconnaissance played a crucial role in two key areas of intelligence gathering: photographic intelligence and electronic intelligence (ELINT). As early as the spring of 1946, USAFE initiated the establishment of a small fleet of RB-26C aircraft, which were intended to be assigned to the 45th Reconnaissance Squadron stationed at Fürth Air Base, near Nürnberg. However, the exact nature of their mission remained shrouded in secrecy. By the summer of that year, this flight became operational and commenced occasional photoreconnaissance missions over the Berlin corridor and border regions. In 1947, the unit relocated to Fürstenfeldbruck AB. As the RB-26 flight expanded in size, it was officially assigned to the 7498th Air Force Squadron in March 1949.

Hunting for radars

The unit also employed ELINT B-17s, which

took a different route to join the operation. In 1946, there were multiple photomapping B-17s stationed at Fürstenfeldbruck. These aircraft belonged to Detachment A (Det A) of the 10th Photo Reconnaissance Group (PRG) and were part of Project Casey Jones. The objective of this project was to create updated maps of Europe and North Africa.

In August 1946, there was significant unrest caused by the shooting down of two USAF C-47s over Yugoslavia. These aircraft had strayed off course on two separate occasions. The USAFE Headquarters in Wiesbaden was curious about how the Yugoslavs were able to effectively intercept the C-47s amidst poor weather conditions.

To investigate further, two Casey Jones

*Project Casey Jones was initiated to obtain photographic coverage for the revision of existing charts and the creation of maps in areas lacking adequate mapping. The mission engaged two bomb groups, the 305th and the 306th Bomb Groups, tasked with covering specific regions, including continental Europe (west of the Russian zone), Iceland, North Africa (up to approximately 50 miles/80.5 kilometers inland from the coasts), the Azores, and the Canary Islands. To accomplish this, the crews utilized modified and converted B-17Gs, flying at high altitudes of 20,000 feet (6,096 meters) or higher above the terrain. Both groups had four squadrons of 12 B-17s each. The B-17s were all stripped of their armament and modified with initially one and later two Fairchild K-17 or KB-18 Reconnaissance and Mapping Cameras.
The photo above is of B-17G 44-83495 from the 306th BG at NAS Port Lyautey in French Morocco in 1946. This B-17 was transferred to Oberpfaffenhofen in 1947 as part of the 10th Headquarters and Base Services Squadron (HBS). Other Casey Jones B-17s operated from the German bases Giebelstadt, Fürstenfeldbruck, and Lechfeld. The photo on the left is of a Casey Jones B-17G of the 305th BG at St. Trond/Brustem, Belgium.
Photo above: USAF/P. A. Schelter.
Photo on the left: USAF/305th BG.*

Chapter One - **All-out intelligence**

B-17s were promptly equipped with specialized ELINT equipment. These aircraft were then tasked to fly so called ferret missions along the Italian-Yugoslav border.

On the very first mission, the B-17 crew had a stroke of luck as the Yugoslavs immediately activated their radars to track the aircraft. It revealed that the Yugoslav Air Force had effectively harnessed radar equipment left behind by the German Luftwaffe's Luftnachrichten-Regiment 248 at various locations.

During World War II, the German air defense had employed advanced radar systems to detect and intercept enemy aircraft. Among these were radar systems code named Mammut, Wassermann, and Jagdschloss, which were used for long-range early warning detection. In contrast, the Würzburg radar, a technologically sophisticated creation of Telefunken, was pivotal for the Luftwaffe's ground-controlled interception operations. The B-17 ELINT operation provided conclusive evidence that the Yugoslavs had successfully restored a World War II-era German Würzburg radar station to operational status. Emboldened by this achievement, the unit proactively undertook flights along the borders of the Iron Curtain and the Berlin corridors with the aim of collecting intelligence on Soviet radar systems. On November 1, 1948, the B-17 component, including photoreconnaissance and ELINT B-17s, became the 7499th Air Force Squadron. Subsequently, on January 10, 1950, the 7499th Squadron absorbed the 7498th Squadron and its RB-26Cs, forming the 7499th Composite Squadron. In August 1950, the covert unit relocated from Fürstenfeldbruck to Wiesbaden Air Base to be closer to the Berlin corridors and the USAFE Headquarters in the city center.

The 7499th Composite Squadron continued its well-established routine of flying missions along the Berlin corridors from its new air base at Erbenheim, near Wiesbaden. Since 2012 this base is known as Lucius D. Clay Kaserne.

Douglas RB-26C Invader 44-35914 "Hot Lips" from the 45th Reconnaissance Squadron parked on the visitors platform of RAF Northolt near London. The Invaders of the 45th operated mostly at night and were pained all black, with the registration in red. Photo: Les Vowles/ABPIC.

The RB-26C, 44-35914, below was assigned to both 7499th CS and 7405th SS from at least 1950 to 1958. It was equipped with split-vertical cameras and concentrated most of its efforts in the Berlin Corridors.
The photo was taken at Wiesbaden AB in 1953. Photo: Bob Brewer via 7499th Group Association.

Chapter One - All-out intelligence

C-97A 49-2592 at Tempelhof Airport, Berlin, in the mid-1950s. With the code name Pie Face, this aircraft was the first specially modified reconnaissance aircraft supplied to the 7499th SS, arriving in 1953. It carried a special 240-inch focal length camera. Like most of its C-97 successors, this aircraft had an open cargo deck, with its special equipment hidden below the deck and in the crew area. The serial number on the tail carries the prefix "o," identifying the plane as over ten years old. This implies that the photograph was taken at Tempelhof sometime after 1959 and 1962, the year the C-97 was deployed to Florida. Photo: Author's collection/via 7499th Group Association. The photo on the right shows C-97A 49-2592 during final approach at Tempelhof in August 1960. Photo: Ralf Manteufel.

Three air corridors

In November 1945, an agreement was signed by the four powers, outlining the use of three air corridors to access Berlin. Each corridor was 20 miles (32 kilometers) wide and led to a 40-mile (64 kilometers) control zone encompassing the city.

The agreement did not impose limitations on the type of aircraft allowed to enter Berlin. However, the Soviet interpretation restricted aerial access for the three Western Allies to solely support their military garrisons stationed in Berlin. Nonetheless, during the 1948 Berlin airlift, cargo aircraft were utilized covertly and equipped with sensors to gather intelligence. These ferret missions often triggered responses from Soviet electronic defenses, which were recorded and analyzed post-mission. Remarkably, valuable

information could be obtained during these operations, as several Soviet air bases were located directly beneath or in proximity to the corridors. Interestingly, no East German units were stationed near these corridors.

The initial air corridor agreement allowed unrestricted aircraft altitude, but the Soviets later demanded a 10,000 (3,048 meters) ceiling, citing safety concerns. The corridors spanned approximately one-sixth of the Soviet zone of occupation. Flying at higher altitudes would enable side-looking cameras to capture images of the entire zone. The imposed 10,000 feet ceiling of the corridors prevented the American and British photoreconnaissance units from achieving far-reaching photography inside the Soviet zone. Instead, peripheral missions along the East German border were undertaken as an alternative. These missions involved flying at significantly higher altitudes, exceeding 30,000 feet (9,144 meters).

Equipped with sophisticated oblique cameras, the reconnaissance planes could efficiently capture images of every corner of the Soviet zone, particularly during favorable weather conditions.

Mock attacks

Although the existing agreement stated that aircraft flying through the corridor should not be challenged by the Soviets, it was a regular occurrence for Soviet fighters to conduct aggressive mock attacks on Allied transport aircraft and civilian airliners. Thankfully, actual firing upon aircraft was rare but did occur in several instances.

In April 1952, a Soviet MiG-15 Fagot attacked an Air France DC-4, which fortunately managed to land safely. However, in March 1953, an RAF Lincoln RF531/C from the Central Gunnery School at RAF Leconfield, which had unintentionally crossed the border near one of the corridors, was shot down. During the same month, a BEA Viking was also attacked by MiGs in one of the corridors. It was under these challenging and perilous circumstances that the USAF carried out their missions.

Unfortunately, there were occasional operational losses as well. On July 30, 1952, the unit lost RB-26C 44-35894 in a crash near Roith, Austria. The four crew members survived but sustained major injuries. They were on a reconnaissance training mission near Innsbruck, flying through a valley formed by steep mountains. While attempting to pull up and exit the valley at the end of the photo run, the aircraft stalled and crashed into the mountain at an altitude of 5,200 feet (1,585 meters), completely breaking apart upon impact.

Another crash occurred a week later, on August 7, 1952. This time, RB-26C 44-35885 crashed four miles southeast of Wiesbaden when one of its engines caught fire during takeoff. The pilot attempted an emergency landing in the Rhine, but unfortunately, two crew members lost their lives in the crash landing.

B-17 phased out

Significant changes occurred within the 7499th Squadron starting in 1951 with the arrival of the first Douglas C-54s. These aircraft included both photoreconnaissance and ELINT variants, gradually replacing the B-17s by 1953. Most of them went through the Big Safari system and were equipped with advanced data collection systems. Being common types of transport aircraft, they had the advantage of blending in with the regular air traffic to and from Berlin.

A little-known fact is that there were also air corridors into Vienna. Vienna, the capital of Austria, found itself in the Soviet-occupied part of the country. To access the city, there were two corridors passing through the Soviet Zone: one from the American Zone in West Germany and another from the north via Italy. Flight operations in these corridors followed similar procedures to those in the Berlin corridors, but there was one significant distinction.

Aircraft were required to land at Tulln Air Base (now Tulln-Langenlebarn), situated 21 miles west of Vienna within the Soviet zone of occupation. This presented a unique challenge in ensuring that Soviet observers and air controllers did not impede the RB-26, C-47, and occasional RB-17 collection missions conducted by the 7499th Squadron. Given the presence of numerous Soviet

In the summer of 1952, at the request of General Lauris Norstad, the commander of USAFE (United States Air Forces in Europe), a secret reconnaissance project was initiated in Europe. The objective was to conduct covert flights within the Berlin air corridors under the guise of routine courier operations. The project was highly classified, leading to the establishment of stringent ground rules. Documentation was kept to a minimum, favoring personal contact and direct communication. Only a select few individuals were informed, and information was strictly distributed on a need-to-know basis. Recognizing the vital importance of the project, no budgetary limits were imposed.

To ensure utmost security, aircraft contractors involved in the project adhered to strict measures, including working in closed-off areas for any modifications. Furthermore, it was agreed that existing aircraft would serve as platforms for the project, eliminating the need for the development of new aircraft. Initially, the project office was authorized for a five-year commitment to provide reconnaissance aircraft specifically for use in the Berlin air corridors within USAFE.

In 1953, it was realized that the project's structure and capabilities lent themselves well to other special reconnaissance initiatives worldwide. Consequently, the project was assigned its own codename, which is still recognized today: Big Safari.

Chapter One - All-out intelligence

Boeing C-97A 49-2592 Pie Face, showcased here in the colors it wore during its assignment to the 7505th Support Squadron, underwent significant modifications. Initially, Boeing equipped prototype YC-97A 45-59590 with the K-42 240-inch oblique camera. The Long Range Oblique Photography (LOROP) conversion took place at the Boeing factory in Seattle, Washington. Following the conversion, the YC-97 underwent a six-week operational evaluation in Europe in early 1952, based at Wiesbaden. During this period, it conducted several reconnaissance flights along the borders of the Iron Curtain, producing positive results despite facing altitude limitations due to being underpowered Subsequently, the C-97A was identified as a more suitable LOROP platform. With a pressurized cabin and more powerful engines, it enabled the LOROP camera—known as "Big Betha"—to operate at higher altitudes, providing enhanced visibility behind the Iron Curtain. The C-97A required a large cutout in the forward upper deck, necessitating structural reinforcements. The camera could be used for vertical and oblique (left and right) photography through a large window behind covert doors. In addition to K-42 camera, the Pie Face C-97 also housed a K-30 100-inch focal length camera and a K-17 trimetrogon system of three mapping cameras.

military targets in this zone, intelligence gathering in these corridors was nearly as crucial as in the more renowned Berlin corridors. The Vienna corridors ceased to exist in 1955 when Austria gained independence, leading to the withdrawal of all allied military forces from the country.

Project Pie Face

During the early 1950s, the USAF initiated a covert program called Big Safari. This program was managed by a logistics command office and served as a platform to develop and oversee various clandestine reconnaissance aircraft projects. Big Safari played a significant role in the inception of nearly every specialized reconnaissance aircraft from 1952 to the present day, including those discussed in the following paragraphs. The USAF developed all of these aircraft through the Big Safari program.

To maintain cover stories, one of the guiding principles of Big Safari was to assign aircraft designators that appeared as innocuous as possible. For instance, the modified C-97 reconnaissance aircraft were officially known simply as C-97s, not as EC-97s or RC-97s. The use of "EC-" and "RC-" designators for these aircraft and the C-130s likely emerged from speculation in various publications targeting the press and aviation enthusiasts.

The initial aircraft to be developed and delivered under Project Big Safari was a C-97A with the serial number 49-2592. It was assigned to the 7499th Squadron in 1953 and carried the project name Pie Face. This Boeing had several cameras fitted aft the cockpit on and beneath the cargo floor. These large cameras were all positioned behind sliding hatches. There was a 100-inch (2540 mm.) K-30 camera and a trio of trimetrogon K-17 cameras.

Enormous camera

But what Pie Face made so special was an enormous 240-inch-focal length (6000 mm.) oblique camera, the largest ever constructed, weighing 6,500 pounds. Initially, the camera was installed in a Convair RB-36, but it was deemed too provocative to conduct clandestine overflights of the Soviet Union with such an aircraft. Instead, it was decided to modify a standard transport aircraft, specifically the C-97, to accommodate the massive camera.

The modification occurred at General Dynamics' Convair Division at Fort Worth, Texas. The huge K-42 camera was nicknamed the Big Thing and Big Bertha by its constructors and had the capability to photograph objects 70 miles away and produced giant 18x36 inch negatives (46 by 91 cm) with exceptional resolution. These negatives were captured on the largest rolls of film ever produced by Kodak.

The camera could be positioned to capture vertical, left, or right oblique photographs through a large window concealed by covert doors. Its power was exemplified by the ability of a photo interpreter to discern a golf ball from an altitude of 45,000 feet (13,716 meters). Unfortunately, the camera's effectiveness was limited by the 10,000 feet (3,048 meters) altitude restriction imposed by the Soviets in the Berlin corridor. Nevertheless, its fine resolution provided valuable, razor sharp intelligence. The C-97 primarily conducted reconnaissance missions along the borders of Eastern European nations. Due to runway limitations at Wiesbaden at the time, the Pie Face C-97 operated from Rhein-Main Air Base as part of Detachment 1, 7499th Squadron; which later became Detachment 1, 7405th Squadron in 1955.

In 1962, C-97 from the Project Pie Face was deployed to Florida to carry out reconnaissance missions off the coast of Cuba at the onset of the Cuban Missile Crisis. It was eventually retired in 1963. In 1964, the camera was donated to the Air Force Museum, along with a contact print of a golf ball on a course.

Special, CIA-type of operations

The covert RB-26s and C-47s continued the Berlin corridor work until 1955. In addition, by 1955, the first C-118A had also arrived with the unit. This aircraft, 51-3822, became part of the 7405th SS. This C-118 and at least two other C-118s were operated and maintained for "another agency", which was presumed to be the CIA. However, These aircraft were never officially assigned to the unit, and it remains unknown what the exact nature of their mission was at Wiesbaden.

According to Henry Bowles Angle, a 1st Lt. Electronic Warfare Officer (EWO) with the 7405th Support Squadron from 1954 to 1957, the C-118s belonged to the C-flight, the special activities flight of the squadron. This was a small flight with only four people, basically, two crews of a pilot and a navigator each. They were involved in what Angle called: "Special CIA-type of operations."

Super-secret by nature

The true nature of the secret CIA operations is still the subject of speculation. To this day, the CIA has not revealed the sinister activities of its flights at Wiesbaden. Details, other than the statement that these were C-118 operations catering to the agency's airlift needs, were then and still are withheld. These transport needs must have been directly related to CIA operations in Europe in the

Between ca. 1955 and 1965 a total of four Douglas C-118A Liftmasters were assigned to the 7405th Support Squadron. Likely, this was only a cover up because the C-188s were used by the Central Intelligence Agency (CIA). The precise nature of the C-118 deployment at Wiesbaden is still largely a mystery. Also a mystery: the CIA painted its C-118s in Germany with spoof serials. The C-118 in the photo taken in September 1965 on Tempelhof wears serial "0-13842". Its real serial number was 51-3823. All the C-flight C-118s in the 7505th SS had bogus serials. Prior to the establishment of the 7405th unit in 1955, there were reports of C-118s operating in West Germany. It seems that C-118A with the serial number 51-3820 was involved in suspicious activities during the 1950s, as it was observed at various airfields in West Germany using the false tail number "0-13838." The suffix "0" holds a special significance in this context. The U.S. serial system follows the U.S. fiscal year of the federal government, during which defense budgets are allocated to manufacturers. For instance, the U.S. fiscal year 1951 began on October 1, 1951, and ended on September 30, 1952. Therefore, the C-118 with the serial number 51-3820 was assigned this serial during the corresponding fiscal year. It is important to note that the serial number reflects the Fiscal Year in which the order for the aircraft is placed, not the year of delivery. The addition of "0" is implemented to prevent duplication and confusion once an aircraft reaches 10 years of age. In this case, the tail code 13820 could also represent the fiscal year 1961. In later years, this system was modified, and the prefix "0" was eliminated. The serial 51-3842 on the C-118 (left) was from a Lockheed RC-121C that crashed during a test flight at Marysville, CA, on March 22, 1961. Photo: Ralf Manteufel.

Chapter One - All-out intelligence

Covert CIA operations from Wiesbaden Air Base

In 1954, the CIA procured seven modified P2V Neptune anti-submarine aircraft for ELINT missions across Europe, Japan, and Taiwan. Under the guise of RB-69s in USAF colors, two planes (serials 54-4038 and 54-4039) were sent to Wiesbaden for test and evaluation in the spring of 1957. In the summer of 1957, they were replaced by 54-4040 and 54-4041. Their deployment occurred in May and June 1957, positioned as Flight D within the 7405th Special Squadron, at least on record. While these aircraft were versatile spy planes equipped with advanced technological apparatus developed at the renowned Skunk Works in Burbank, California, the official description dubbed the blue-black RB-69s as "radio trainers." They possessed intricate equipment for electronic intelligence border surveillance tasks. It is reported that the RB-69s at Wiesbaden featured tube-like antennas on either side of the fuselage, likely an early iteration of Side Looking Airborne Radar (SLAR). These planes also boasted an innovative and highly effective leaflet dispersal system. Moreover, the aircraft were designed to drop supplies or personnel through a specialized hatch cut into the aircraft's underside. This hatch could be opened during flight for this specific purpose. Notably, this feature was intended for utilization over Eastern Bloc territories rather than friendly regions.

During the Cold War, the CIA frequently utilized Rhein-Main's facilities, particularly those in Wiesbaden, which made sense due to the CIA's headquarters being situated within the vast I.G. Farben office complex in nearby Frankfurt.

From Wiesbaden, the CIA operated several Douglas C-118s for covert transport missions. The proximity of USAFE headquarters and the 497th Reconnaissance Technical Group at Schierstein/Wiesbaden likely contributed to the air base's consistent use for covert operations. The 497th offered intelligence support to flying units in Europe during the Cold War, providing target information, film development tools, and photo interpretation. The USAF provided effective cover for clandestine activities, exemplified by Detachment A, referred to as "Weather Reconnaissance Squadron (Provisional) - 1 (WRSP-1)" to conceal its true identity.

Detachment A originated at the Watertown Strip, also known as Groom Lake, in Southern Nevada, now famously recognized as the supersecret Area 51. In April 1956, this covert CIA unit relocated to RAF Lakenheath, England. There, two U-2s were dismantled at Groom Lake and transported via Douglas C-124s to form Detachment A, the first of three, at RAF Lakenheath.

By May 4, personnel and equipment, including the two aircraft, had arrived in England. The National Advisory Committee on Aeronautics (NACA) released a declassified U-2 cover story stating that a Lockheed-developed aircraft would be flown by the USAF Air Weather Service to study high-altitude phenomena. On May 21, 1956, the first U-2 flight from Lakenheath took place. However, due to political considerations—owing to the British government's awareness of its true purpose—no operational missions occurred from Lakenheath. Consequently, on June 15, Detachment A moved to Wiesbaden Air Base in the U.S. military zone, where political constraints were absent and even the Germans were uninformed.

Just five days later, on June 20, 1956, CIA pilot Carl Overstreet launched Project Aquatone, under which clandestine operations behind the Iron Curtain were executed. Numerous flights followed over the Soviet Union, which meant that these remarkable aircraft attracted much public attention at one of the busiest U.S. air bases in Europe. Therefore, by October 1956, Detachment A relocated again, this time to Giebelstadt Air Base near Würzburg, closer to the East German border and mostly out of public view.

At Wiesbaden, the CIA's Air Division of DD/P (Department of the Deputy Director of Plans) trained foreign pilots, including displaced persons and repatriated refugees passing through German military processing centers. Czech and Polish airmen, some of whom were drawn from a significant pool of veterans in England who had escaped from Poland during WWII, were assigned to a staging base operated by the CIA in Athens, Greece, likely Elefsina Air Base. From here, they flew missions with 7499th RB-26 aircraft, engaging in leaflet drops over Albania, Bulgaria, and Hungary. Encouraged by the outcomes, the CIA once again turned to stateless Poles in 1957 when crews were required for a covert operation involving two Lockheed RB-69A (P2V-7U) Neptunes, which were on loan from the U.S. Navy.

Under the code name Project Ostiary, these crews conducted clandestine missions along and within the Eastern Bloc, based out of Wiesbaden, Germany.

Hot Pepper C-54D 43-17248 was modified to operate a 100-inch focal length K-30 camera. This camera captured images through hatches located on each side of the fuselage directly behind the cockpit. The hatches consisted of 24-inch by 48-inch rapid-action doors that were operated pneumatically. The doors blended perfectly with the fuselage and were practically invisible for detection. A 16-inch K-7 camera for downward photomapping was mounted directly behind the nose wheel. The C-54, which conducted almost daily missions flying the Berlin corridors to Tempelhof, was also packed with covert ELINT equipment. Some of the equipment was covertly installed in the AN/APS-23 radome beneath the aircraft. It also had antennas in the vertical stabilizer for an APR-9 Early Warning Radar receiver in the tail section. In March 1962, the U.S. Air Force declared the aircraft surplus and withdrew it from use—on paper, that is. However, the C-54 had been in the USAF factory #4 at the General Dynamics facility in Fort Worth since January 20, 1962, where it was prepared for a new mission in Southeast Asia. Under the codename Hilo Hattie and carrying the false registration 43-17235, borrowed from a C-54 that was Struck off Charge in 1948, its primary Asian mission was mapping the Vietnam/Cambodia border area and locating enemy base areas using infrared cameras. The photo is taken by the German photographer Ralf Manteufel during the U.S. Armed Forces Day on May 20, 1961, at Tempelhof Air Base.

1950s—flying agents and diplomats back and forth and performing courier services on behalf of U.S. embassies. They were possibly transporting innocent-looking cargo, the true nature of which was unknown, but as liaison aircraft, they were actually involved in the super-secret U-2 overflight programs conducted by the CIA at that time. A glimpse of this mystery emerged in 1957 when C-118 51-3822 was brutally shot down by Soviet fighters over Armenia—a subject that will be explored further in chapter three of this book.

Establishment of 7499th Support Group

Over time, as the Cold War advanced and the demands for intelligence, along with the technological resources to meet them, became more intricate, the 7499th Squadron underwent expansion, evolving into the 7499th Support Group. This transformation took place on May 10, 1955, resulting in the establishment of three subordinate squadrons, each assigned distinct responsibilities. The first of these squadrons was the 7405th Support Squadron (SS), with three flights entrusted with conducting ELINT missions (A-flight), photoreconnaissance missions (B-flight), and supporting mysterious CIA operations (C-flight). The ELINT missions were initially carried out only along the outer boundaries of the Iron Curtain, spanning from the Baltic to the Adriatic and the Black Sea. The C-54s of the B-flight mainly conducted photo missions in the Berlin corridors.

The second unit, named the 7406th SS, specialized in flying missions focused on Communications Intelligence (COMINT) along the Eastern Bloc's borders, operating in regions similar to those covered by the 7405th squadron, albeit not within the corridors.

The third entity, the 7407th SS, engaged in high-altitude photoreconnaissance missions, including the execution of two denied territory overflight programs. Both of these units operated from Rhein-Main, with the 7407th maintaining a Detachment at Bitburg Air Force Base which operated three RF-100 special photoreconnaissance Super Sabres under the project name Slick Shick. In the early 1970s, the Group with the 7406th and the 7407th would be inactivated, but the 7405th would carry on its specialized corridor and Iron Curtain missions during the remaining years of the Cold War.

Chapter One - All-out intelligence

Aircraft known assigned to 7499th AFS, 7499th CS and 7499th SG

Serial number	Type/model	Description/background
42-72465	Douglas C-54D	A veteran of the 1948 Berlin Airlift. Assigned to the 7499th CS by September 1951 and remained active until being transferred to the 7405th SS on May 10, 1955. Prior to its transfer, 42-72465 and 42-72667 were converted to ELINT standard as part of Project Pretty Girl by General Dynamics at the USAF's strategic Plant-4 Fort Worth. The C-54 continued operations until it was withdrawn from use and assigned to the Military Aircraft Storage and Disposition Center (MASDC) on July 10, 1966, where it eventually was scrapped.
42-72667	Douglas C-54D	A veteran of the 1948 Berlin Airlift. Part of Project Pretty Girl. Assigned to the 7499th SG by August 1951 and reassigned to the 7405th SS on May 10, 1955.
42-93526	Douglas C-47A	Assigned to the Wiesbaden Air Base base flight, but on loan to the 7499th CS for a few weeks in October and November 1950.
43-15521	Douglas C-47A	Assigned to the 7499th CS by July 1952. Went to the 7405th SS in May 1955.
43-17248	Douglas C-54D	A veteran of the 1948 Berlin Airlift. Converted to photo recce standard as part of Project Hot Pepper and assigned to the 7499th CS by August 1950. Transferred to the 7405th SS on May 10, 1955. The C-54 was at General Dynamics, Fort Worth, several times for modifications. Apparently, in 1962, this aircraft was re-serialled as 43-17235. Several special mission aircraft were temporarily given serials of standard aircraft to allow them to infiltrate for spying/reconnaissance missions along the Berlin corridors. The plane is now preserved and on display at Donaldson AFB, South Carolina.
43-39021	Boeing B-17G	Was assigned to the 45th RS at Fürstenfeldbruck, West Germany, on January 21, 1948. Assigned to the 7499th Air Force Squadron (AFS), Fürstenfeldbruck, on November 2, 1948, and redesignated RB-17G on March 22, 1949. Transferred to Wiesbaden on August 25, 1950 and remained active until June 29, 1953, when it was assigned to Air Material Command and moved to the Mobile Air Material Area at Brookley Field, AL, on July 9, 1953.
43-48241	Douglas C-47D	Flew with the unit between at least September 1952 and October 1954.
44-8846	Boeing RB-17G	Flew six combat missions over Germany in 1945 with the 351st Bombardment Group (aircraft's nickname Half Pint), assigned to Project Casey Jones. Went in 1947 to 45th RS at Fürstenfeldbruck, West Germany, early in 1947 to conduct ELINT missions along the borders of the Iron Curtain and in the Berlin air corridors. Redesignated RB-17G, it was assigned to the 7499th AFS on November 1, 1948. On August 25, 1950 is was transferred to Wiesbaden, West Germany, and assigned to the 7150th Air Base Group. On July 23, 1951, assignment followed to the 7499th CS until it was transferred to Ogden Air Material Area (AMA) at Hill AFB, UT, in December 1953. After demilitarization, the aircraft was Struck off Charge (SOC) in August 1954 and sold to the Institut Géographique Nationale (IGN) at Creil, France, as F-BGSP in December 1954. It was Withdrawn From Use (WFU) in 1959 and stored. While with the IGN, it spent some time in South Africa as ZS-DXM. In May 1985, it was transferred to the Forteresse Toujours Volante Association, part of the flying museum Jean-Baptiste Salis at Aérodrome de Cerny-la Ferté-Alais, France. It was re-registered as F-AZDX, firstly as Lucky Lady and later as Pink Lady, before being finally grounded in 2010 and put on display in the Jean-Bapiste Museum.
44-8889	Boeing RB-17G	Served in Europe in 1945 but was stored until it had been assigned to the 7499th CS by April 1949. It was converted as an ELINT aircraft (RB-17G) and served until September 1953, when it was returned to the USA for rework at the Mobile Air Depot at Brookley Field, AL. In August 1954, it was sold to the Institut Geographique Nationale (IGN) at Creil, France, as F-BGSO. it was heavily modified by the IGN for survey work. On September 1976, the aircraft was presented to the Musée de l'Air at Le Bourget and remains in storage there.
44-8891	Boeing RB-17G	Was assigned to Project Casey Jones, photomapping and intelligence gathering flights over Europe and North Africa. Operated out of Istres, France, and Marrakech, French Morocco in 1945/46. Assigned to the 45th RS, Fürstenfeldbruck, West Germany, on January 21, 1948. Assigned to the 7499th AFS, Fürstenfeldbruck on November 2, 1948. Redesignated as RB-17G, it was assigned to the 7499th CS, Fürstenfeldbruck, on May 17, 1949 and transferred to Wiesbaden on August 25, 1950. It was assigned to the 5th AD, Strategic Air Command, at Sidi Slimane Air Base, Rabat-Salé, Morocco, on January 3, 1952. Redesignated TB-17G, it moved to the 3918th Air Base Group at RAF Upper Heyford, England, on June 29, 1952. A year later, on August 31, 1953, it was assigned to the Air Material Command, and via Brookley Field, AL, it was sold to the Brazilian Air Force as FAB 5107 in 1954.
44-8895	Boeing B-17G	Assigned to the 45th RS in May 1948 and moved to the 7499th AFS on November 1, 1948. Damaged in a hard landing in August 1949 and withdrawn from use; scrapped in October 1949.
44-34415	Douglas B-26B	Previously served with 45th RS and assigned to 7499th SG on November 1, 1948. No further details about European operations. It was used in clandestine CIA operations in Cuba and participated in the Bay of Pigs operation. It wore the civil registration N5002X, and was with Air America as N46598. It was used in covert CIA missions in Thailand, Vietnam, and Laos.

Serial number	Type/model	Description/background
44-34416	Douglas TB-26B	Assigned to 7499 SS from at least September 1954; transferred to 7405th SS on May 10, 1955. Used for training purposes.
44-34450	Douglas RB-26C	Assigned to 7499th CS from mid-1950; transferred to 7405th SS on May 10, 1955. Withdrawn from use in 1957. Back to the U.S. via Fairey Aviation, Ringway, Manchester the same year.
44-34474	Douglas B-26B	Technically not assigned to 7499 CS, but was attached to its forerunner 45th RS when the aircraft was damaged in a landing accident at Fürstenfeldbruck on February 13, 1948, and scrapped later.
44-35343	Douglas RB-26C	Previously with 1st TRS but reassigned to 7499 CS in July 1953. She was transferred to the 7405th SS on May 10, 1955.
44-35885	Douglas RB-26C	Assigned to the 7499th CS by May 1950; lost in a crash in the Rhine River on August 7, 1952.
44-35894	Douglas RB-26C	Assigned to the 7499th CS by January 1951; lost in a crash in Austria on July 20, 1952.
44-35914	Douglas RB-26C	Assigned to the 7499th CS by May 1950 at least. Transferred to 7405th SS on May 10, 1955.
44-77222	Douglas RC-47D	Went to RAF as Dakota IV KP252 in July 1945. Returned to USAFE on September 22, 1948. Was active with the 7499th CS by June 1949 and most likely was one of the early ELINT aircraft. Quoted as an "RC-47" in a 1950s squadron history records. Remained active until May 1952.
44-83282	Boeing RB-17G	Came from the 10th Headquarters and Base Service Squadron, Oberpfaffenhofen Air Base, when it was assigned to 45th Reconnaissance Squadron, Fürstenfeldbruck Air Base on January 21, 1948. Assigned to 7499th Air Force Squadron, Fürstenfeldbruck Air Base on November 2, 1948. Redesignated RB-17G on March 22, 1949, and assigned to 7499th CS, Wiesbaden Air Base on September 19, 1950. Withdrawn from use on May 25, 1953. Converted to QB-17G standard (drone) at Brookley Field, Alabama. Expended over the White Sands Proving Grounds, Alamogordo, New Mexico, on January 17, 1955.
44-83373	Boeing B-17G	After wandering along the 10th Headquarters and Base Service Squadron, Oberpfaffenhofen Air Base, the 501st Air Service Group, the 7160th Air Base Group, the 165th Composite Group, and the 60th Air Base Group all at Wiesbaden Air Base, this B-17 finally was assigned to the 7499th CS at Fürstenfeldbruck Air Base on September 19, 1949. It was first designated TB-17G and RB-17G on February 6, 1950. In 1953 the Fortress was withdrawn from use and returned to the USA on March 9, 1956. Converted to drone, it was redesignated QB-17N on January 17, 1957. Its last assignment was the Air Proving Ground Center, Air Research and Development Command, Eglin AFB, Valparaiso, Florida, where it was expended on May 26, 1958.
44-83378	Boeing RB-17G	Came from the 10th Headquarters and Base Service Squadron, Oberpfaffenhofen Air Base, when it was assigned to the 7499th Air Force Squadron at Fürstenfeldbruck on January 19, 1949. The Fortress was redesignated RB-17G before it was transferred to the 7499th CS at Wiesbaden Air Base on August 25, 1950. Following a taxying accident on September 26, 1950, it returned to U.S. where it remained active until transfer to Força Aérea Brasileira as 5410 on May 1, 1955.
49-2592	Boeing C-97A	Converted to Pie Face reconnaissance aircraft and began operation with the 7499th CS in 1953.

Lineage 7499th Support Group

Designated as the 7499th Air Force Squadron and organized on November 1, 1948.
Redesignated as 7499th Composite Squadron in 1949.
Redesignated as 7499th Support Squadron in 1954.
Redesignated as 7499th Support Group on May 10, 1955.
Inactivated on June 30, 1974 (7405th SS assumes mission of the inactivated group).

Before C-97A 53-0106 came to the 7405th SS in 1965, the aircraft was part of CIA projects and was involved in the extensive CIA electronic intelligence activity called Project Quality ELINT, carried out by the CIA Office of ELINT (OEL). It employed a variety of aircraft to gather data on radars operated by the Soviet Union, China, East Germany, and Cuba. Between August 1963 and October 1966, a combination of Air Force RB-47H, C-97, and C-135 aircraft conducted missions carrying OEL's Power and Pattern Measurement System (PPMS). The PPMS gathered data on the Soviet air defense and guidance radars. It provided useful information to further improve the U.S. stealth developments. Under the Big Safari program, C-97A 53-0106 was configured for ELINT collection aimed at the Soviet SA-2 missile system. Under the code name Wine Sap, the covert aircraft conducted missions in the Berlin Corridors using advanced scientific and technical equipment to collect emitter information. From 1970, under the new code name Rivet Stock, it collected information about the new Soviet missile SA-4 radar system. Amongst other electronic gadgets, it had retractable Direction Finding (DF) antennas in each wingtip. Photo: Ralf Manteufel.

Chapter Two

Dancing the Corridors

In the aftermath of the 7499th's extensive reorganization, a momentous transformation took place on May 10, 1955. The 7405th Support Squadron undertook the critical responsibility of vigilantly patrolling Berlin's intricate air corridors, building on the legacy of its predecessor, the 7499th Support Squadron.

The squadron's fleet included various aircraft types within its operational arsenal. Among these were the versatile TB-26C and B-26C Invaders, robust transport aircraft such as the C-47, C-54D, and RC-54D, along with the large dynamic C-97A. Moreover, the CIA's C-118A operated secretly from a remote and heavily guarded corner of Wiesbaden Air Base.

Berlin Air Corridor missions, distinguished by the versatile use of aircraft, epitomized the squadron's operations. Most of these aircraft had a nondescript appearance reminiscent of conventional transport aircraft. Under this unassuming facade, these aircraft demonstrated adeptness in various intelligence-gathering roles. One fascinating aspect was the deliberate omission of conspicuous radar protrusions or antennas, or hiding them away as much as possible, hiding their true mission at first glance.

Transport aircraft in disguise

Each aircraft was tailored for covert flights in the corridor or along the borders of the Iron Curtain. Virtually every plane was different. Innocent on the outside, stuffed inside with cutting-edge scientific and technical equipment for covert reconnaissance tasks without attracting Soviet attention. The 7405th gradually developed strategic prowess and employed ingenious methods for photography missions. Cameras were discreetly stored behind specially designed panels that could be quickly and conveniently opened in flight. ELINT equipment was hidden in innocuous-looking retractable radar domes. The integration of cameras and sophisticated electronic equipment was so unobtrusive that their presence could only be ascertained by internal aircraft inspections. The squadron's activities were obscured by a veneer of routine work, with pilots adhering to the usual flight plans and routinely obtaining clearance from air traffic control. This camouflage artfully maintained its disguise as a nondescript transport aircraft and provided a seamless continuation of their covert activities.

Unexpected discovery

However, the squadron's scope of operations extended beyond the Berlin air corridors alone. Their operational agenda encompassed a wider area, including involvement in a U.S. Navy operation in July and August 1956. This operation was aimed at photographically capturing Soviet Navy ships crossing the Baltic Sea en route to or returning from the Atlantic and the North Sea. The squadron's Hot Pepper C-54 aircraft were used for this purpose, supplemented by several ELINT missions that captured and kept a sharp eye on the electronics of these ships. Notable was an incident within this operation in which a camera-equipped C-47 was sent to Norway. This mission was intended to record the goodwill port visit of a Soviet naval vessel, which was high on the U.S. priority list. Unfortunately, the visit was disrupted by cloudy weather, making it impossible to collect much imagery.

Coincidentally, a crew member of the C-47 stumbled upon high-quality film newsreel footage showing the ship's visit. This unexpected discovery captured many precise details. So, it was no surprise that the USAF quickly obtained a copy of this priceless footage for further examination.

Akin to pioneering

Such events marked the early years of the spy unit at Wiesbaden. It was serious business the specialists were engaged in, but it was also akin to pioneering. Aircraft were provisionally fitted with reconnaissance equipment, and the crews often did not take the Eastern Bloc's borders very closely at first. That soon changed when the Soviet defense showed its teeth. It was not until years later that Electronic Warfare Officer Henry Bowles Angle, who flew 200 ferret missions, told how it was like at the 7405th. With a degree in industrial economics under his belt, he enlisted in 1952 in the USAF Electronic Warfare education program for college graduates. Via Scott Air Force Base, he ended up at Ellington Air Force Base, where he graduated in Navigation, Weather, and Electronic Countermeasures in 1953. As a 2nd Lt. Observer, he was deployed to Europe in late 1953.

Most of his fellow students went to assignments in the Far East, many in Japan, but Henry was married, and his wife was a teacher of the German language, so that was convenient for a deployment to Germany. He was assigned to the 10th Tactical Reconnaissance Group at Spangdahlem, where he was to fly as an Electronic Counter Measurement (ECM) on the RB-26C. But it did not come to that for him. Instead, the USAFE HQ-base Wiesbaden became his destination. He joined the 7499th Composite Squadron.

risk of straying over the nearby border was, therefore, great.

"What are the alternatives?"

At Wiesbaden, he first received a briefing tives?" Henry wanted to know. The TSCO replied that he was the first to ask about this, "I don't re

Three RB-26Cs from the 10th Tactical Reconnaissance Group (TRG) at Spangdahlem Air Base, Germany. Several RB-26s from the group went to the 7499th, like RB-26C Invader, serial number 44-35343. This RB-26C was assigned to the 1st Tactical Reconnaissance Squadron (TRS) at Toul Air Base in France in 1952, but following the transfer of the 1st TRS to Spangdahlem in May 1953, the Invader was assigned to the 7499th CS in July 1953. Photo: U.S. Air Force.

Chapter Two - Dancing the corridors

ally know. But I don't think they are going to be good." Voluntary was a stretch. So Henry ended up with the secret reconnaissance squadron where he was assigned to the duo of C-54s that, when Henry arrived at Wiesbaden, took over the duties of the B-17 ELINT planes. These were veterans of Operation Vittles in 1948 used for hauling coal during the airlift. Carbon was everywhere, and after a turbulent flight, the "back-enders," as the ELINT specialists on board were called, exited the plane as if they had visited a coal mine.

Pretty Girls along the borders

Henry recalled that after modification, the C-54 participated in the Pretty Girl ELINT-project. According to Henry, that name was chosen because of the large blisters underneath the fuselage of both aircraft, which housed DF antennas. The C-54s (serials 42-72667 and 42-72465) were further equipped with search antennas at the wing ends and a spiral search antenna which was mounted in vertical stabilizer. Furthermore, in addition to the crew of six (two pilots, two navigators, a crew chief, and a flight engineer), there were seven positions for back-enders. Little had been done to hide the external modifiers. It probably did not have to since the C-54 was not used in the Berlin corridor but exclusively for peripheral ferret missions, finding out information of the Soviet radar defense.

The Pretty Girl project gathered all kinds of information about the Soviet radars, which was published in a top-secret Pentagon weekly newsletter about the Soviet electronic order of battle. "We were assigned for missions along the borders of the Iron Curtain, from Baltics to the Black Sea; East Germany, Czechoslovakia, Hungary, Bulgaria, Romania, all the way down to Athens and sometimes to French Marocco," Henry remembered. Each week, they did one or two missions of up to 10 hours. The C-54s were slow — 170 to 210 miles/h— which was a real disadvantage in case of pursuit, but on the other hand, it could stay on its track for lenghty periods of time, and there was a lot of time to work the signals and do 15-20 radar bearings at the same time. C-54s had no pressure cabin; on flights over the Alps, the men on board had to use oxygen. Typical for Europe, the weather was often bad, which forced the C-54s to fly higher than the standard 10,000 feet. And that made flying along the borders with the risk of navigation errors a tricky, dangerous mission.

A horrible situation over the Alps

One time, during a mission in bad weather with hefty turbulence over the Alps, the C-54 Henry was flying in was tossed all over the place. Actually, when the inner lining came down, and the cargo door blew open, he was so scared that he was ready to jump off the plane with his

The Douglas C-118 Liftmaster is an early Cold War-era transport aircraft. The development started in 1944 when the U.S. forces required a more capable version of the C-54 Skymaster. As WWII ended, no military orders were placed, but civilian production started in 1946 as a passenger plane under the name DC-6. In the early 1950s, military interest was renewed, and many C-118s served well into the 1960s.

The C-118 with serial number 51-3822 was attached to the 7405th, which means it was operated by the CIA and maintained by the 7405th. Interestingly, the maintenance summary of July 1958 simply mentions 51-3822 as being 'transferred,' without referencing the MiG encounter behind the Iron Curtain on June 27, 1958.

Michel Debarre

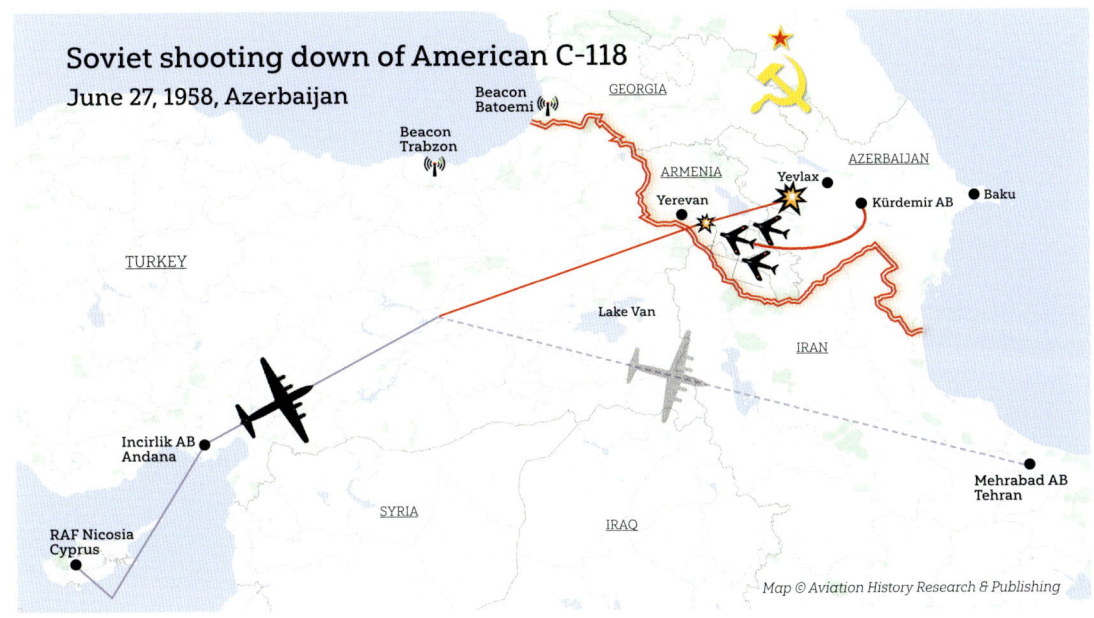

The C-118 51-3822 was supposed to follow a route that would lead south of Lake Van, passing the Iranian border north of Iraq. Instead, the C-118 took a course northeast, passing Lake Van to the north and heading towards Yerevan, Armenia. Eventually, the C-118 was shot at by MiG-17 Fresco fighters from the Baku Red Banner Air Defense District—most likely from the 976th Fighter Air Regiment PVO (Air Defense) at Kürdemir, Azerbaijan. In 2004, the CIA released some of its own findings on the shooting down. According to the CIA, the C-118 was flying by dead reckoning because of weather. The agency suspected that the Soviet beacon at Batumi in Armenia was overriding the Turkish beacon at Trabzon in a deliberate effort to lure the aircraft off course

parachute. To avoid crashing down, they had to escape this horrible situation, and in order to maintain enough altitude to get safely out of the turbulence, they had to divert into Czechoslovakia. Luckily, the Soviet air defense did not come into action, probably because, even for them, the weather conditions were too bad to conduct an intercept at all. "In general, we tried to avoid violating the border, but several times, we came across when we shouldn't have," Henry admitted.

The radar navigator on board a ferret flight would take a radar photo of the position every five minutes; this fix would be logged by the DR-navigator (dead reckoning). This would give an accurate position of the plane, which was an absolute necessity because the ferrets would fly only three miles from the border. But because the C-54 was so slow, sometimes with a heavy headwind, it would not go over 100 miles/h (161 km/h) groundspeed, the drift was significant, and the risk of straying over the nearby border was, therefore, great.

What was C-118 doing in Armenia?

And such a navigational error was easily made. This happened, for example, on June 27, 1958, when one of the CIA's C-118 from Wiesbaden was fired upon by MiGs over Armenia and made an emergency landing on a small airfield over the Azerbaijan border. Nine Americans—including senior USAF officers and members of the CIA—were arrested and taken to Baku for questioning. A diplomatic riot was born. Now, things ended with a hissy fit, as the Russians apparently did not discover the true identity of the party. The nine were released a short time later. After which, speculation began. What was the C-118 doing there? In the afternoon on June 27, 1958, the CIA aircraft, C-118A 51-3822, originating from Flight C, attached to the 7405th at Wiesbaden, left Incilik Air Base, Turkey. That was where the U-2 Detach-

The Soviet Air Defense (PVO) scrambled three MiG-17 Fresco interceptors. They attacked the C-118 with their 30 mm guns, setting fire to the no.2 inboard engine in the left wing of the unarmed aircraft. Photo: PVO.

Chapter Two - Dancing the corridors

> **SOVIET MIGS Fired On Ship, Which Came Down In Fiery Rush**
>
> **Nine Fliers Arrive In Germany After 10-Day Arrest In Russia**
>
> WIESBADEN, Germany, July 8 (AP) — Nine U. S. airmen returned from 10 days detention in the Soviet Union today with the story of how their unarmed transport landed in flames after being fired upon by MIG fighters.
>
> Five of the men bailed out of the burning plane. The other four were fired upon as they were about to land.
>
> The kisses, hugs and tears of families of five of the men greeted them here. All the weary crew were flown here after being turned over to American authorities in Iran by Soviet officials yesterday.
>
> All appeared to be in good shape, although Airman 2/c Peter N. Sabo of Chicago was said to be suffering second-degree burns.
>
> Airman 2/c Earl H. Reamer of St. Louis Park, Minn., had a shaved spot on one side of his head, indicating he had suffered a minor injury.
>
> Because of the men's fatigue, Air Force officers postponed until tomorrow the news conference that had been arranged for the returned fliers.
>
> **GIVES FIRST ACCOUNT**
>
> But the Air Force gave their first account of the plane's forced landing on June 27 while on a flight with supplies from Wiesbaden to Pakistan.
>
> The story:
>
> The big C118 transport strayed across the Soviet border in bad weather and was intercepted by two Soviet MIG jet fighters at 15,000 feet.
>
> The plane was set afire by the first shots from the MIGs. Five crew members took to their parachutes, but the other four remained aboard to ride the plane to a landing.
>
> "With five parachutes in the air and the aircraft in flames the Soviet planes made another firing pass on the crippled plane when it was on the final approach for a forced landing," the Air Force account said.
>
> "The burning plane exploded on the ground shortly after the crew members were able to reach safety."
>
> The Air Force added that the landing wheels were down, indicating readiness for landing, when the MIGs made their second pass.
>
> **TRANSPORT LANDS**
>
> The transport landed on a crude airstrip 75 miles east-southeast of Lake Sevan, which is about half way between the Caspian and Black Seas.

ment B was based at the time. But that morning, the C-118 was also observed at RAF Nicosia on Cyprus. Without an official flight plan and with the cargo and destination undisclosed, the mysterious C-118 took off heading eastward.

We know now that the destination was Tehran, where a stopover was planned, and the flight would continue to Pakistan. Somewhere over the Euphrates Lake area and flying at 15,000 feet (4.572 meters), it went wrong. Trying to bypass a bad weather area, the C-118 ended north of Lake Van while it should have passed south. A greater-than-expected tailwind made things worse and blew them off course. As a result, the Americans inevitably ended up near Yerevan, Armenia, which was passed some 40 miles (circa 65 kilometers) south. Without noticing it, the Americans flew into Russian air space. And that was promptly detected by Russian Air Defense, which immediately scrambled three MiG-17s. An orderly interception and escorted landing were out of the question because, without warning, they immediately opened fire.

Meanwhile, the C-118 had already flown on to a point where Azerbaijan came in sight. After another burst of fire, the fate of the C-118 was sealed because it caught fire in the left wing. Five crew members bailed out, while four remained in the burning plane to its crash landing. After the incident, speculation began about the C-118's crude cargo. It was said to have consisted of secret documents about U.S./British U-2 operations in the Middle East and imminent activities in Pakistan. There, preparations were being made from Peshawar for British spy U-2 flights over Russia.

Specifically, it would have been a briefcase that would have contained the highly classified documents. Given that the nine crew members were released a short time later, it suggests that the Russians did not find any compromising items. Or at least they did not let it appear that way.

Nuclear cruise missiles

While the U.S. kept a close eye on Russian developments in the defense field with ELINT, COMINT, and PHOTINT activities in order to get a good picture of Soviet strength, the U.S. itself did not leave itself indifferent in terms of defense construction in Europe. A particular development in the early years of the Cold War was that of the pilotless bomber. The USAF was building on the developments in Germany during the war with the V-1 "buzz bomb."

The Glenn Martin company was awarded a contract in 1946 to develop the cruise missile. The result was the Martin B-61 surface-to-surface (S.S.) tactical missile, which was capable of carrying either a conventional or nuclear warhead. Launched from a mobile 40-foot trailer by a booster rocket that fell away, the Matador, as the weapon was called, continued toward its target powered by a GE/Allison J-33 jet engine, the same engine that was used in the Lockheed T-33 jet trainer. Unlike the V-1, however, the Matador was controlled electronically from the ground during flight. Its first launch took place in January 1949. Five years later, in March 1954, the 1st Pilotless Bomber Squadron was assigned to the 36th Fighter Bomber Wing (FBW) at Bitburg Air Base, Germany, making it the first operational U.S. missile unit. The 1st PBS was equipped with the B-61A Matador, which could be armed with the W5 nuclear warhead. In the first half of the 1950s, the USAF started fielding more Matador and Mace tactical guided missile squadrons in Europe.

Fire-and-forget

The TM-61A Matador, which had a range of about 200 miles, relied on positive guidance control by radar-directed ground controllers, but they proved to be very susceptible to electronic countermeasures. In late 1954, the USAF added a LORAN-like (Long-range Navigation) guidance system called Shanicle and redesignated the missile TM-61C. In this system, the missile automatically flew a hyperbolic grid. Based upon the results of the TM-61Cs test launched, the USAF calculated the missile's overall reliability at 71 percent and a Circular Error of Probability (CEP) of 1,600 feet (487 meters). But Shanicle still limited the range of TM-61C to that of line-of-sight transmissions; moreover, this guidance system could be jammed. In order to solve this, a special ATRAN (Automatic Terrain Recognition And Navigation) system was developed for the TM-61B, nicknamed Mace. During its development phase, the TM-61B evolved into the TM-76A Mace missile. With 1,400 miles (2,253 kilometers), this fire-and-forget missile had a much greater range. The Mace missile, later redesignated MGM-13A in 1964, was introduced into service in the USAFE in 1959. Tactical missile squadrons became operational at Hahn, Sembach, and Bitburg by 1962. The MGM-13 remained operational in Europe until 1969, when the last Mace squadron was inactivated at Bitburg Air Base.

Follow the terrain

ATRAN relied upon a film loaded into the missile's guidance system. While in flight, the missile's onboard computer would compare the features of the actual terrain with that on the film strip and would eventually lead the missile to its target without any remote control. A rather intriguing fact was that, in order to create these film strips, sand models were made featuring all the terrain features.

A major role in obtaining the necessary data was played by the capture of tons of German mapping and geodesic data after WWII. Where this data was not sufficient, the missing pieces had to be obtained with the help of conventional means, that is manned aircraft. Presumably, the terrain along the missile's flight path over enemy territory was just educated guesswork! In order to obtain up-to-date information to create these sand models, aerial reconnaissance missions were flown over Western Europe, the main area of employment of these missiles. Gathering the missing pieces became the responsibility of the 7499th Support Group.

Lulu Belle and Half Track

Aerial reconnaissance missions for data collection were conducted from Rhein-Main Air Base. In response to the specific needs of these reconnaissance tasks, Headquarters USAFE in

An operational TM-61A nuclear cruise missile during an exercise in the Fifties somewhere in the Hünsruck area near Hahn Air Base in Germany. Photo: U.S. Air Force

Douglas C-54D 47-2684 was modernized under the Big Safari program at the General Dynamics' Fort Worth facility in Texas. As Lulu Belle, the C-54 was equipped with radar and ATRAN equipment to collect cruise missile flight path data in Europe.

Chapter Two - Dancing the corridors

Wiesbaden initiated a project with the codename Aunt Sue under the auspices of the 7499th Support Group There were two squadrons assigned to this project, which had various missions, including ATRAN. The 7405th Support Squadron utilized a Douglas C-54D aircraft (serial number 42-72684) in Project Lulu Belle to gather ATRAN material, while the 7406th Support Squadron employed three Boeing RB-50Ds (serial numbers 48-0107, 48-0307, and 48-0312) in Project Half Track for data collection. Under the Big Safari program, the Lulu Belle C-54D (serial number 53-72684) had an early-generation infrared system installed called a Terrain Reconnaissance Device (TRD), along with an APS-27 active pulse search radar with moving target indicator (MTI). These systems were installed at General Dynamics in Fort Worth, Texas, and Goodyear in Akron, Ohio, which also installed the ATRAN system (the modified navigation radar and camera).

All of this occurred in 1955, and the aircraft arrived at Wiesbaden Air Base in December of that year. In the first half of 1956, Lulu Belle flew at least twenty ATRAN missions. Initially, the quality of the flight lines produced was unacceptable, but it gradually improved as the equipment became more reliable and the crews more proficient.

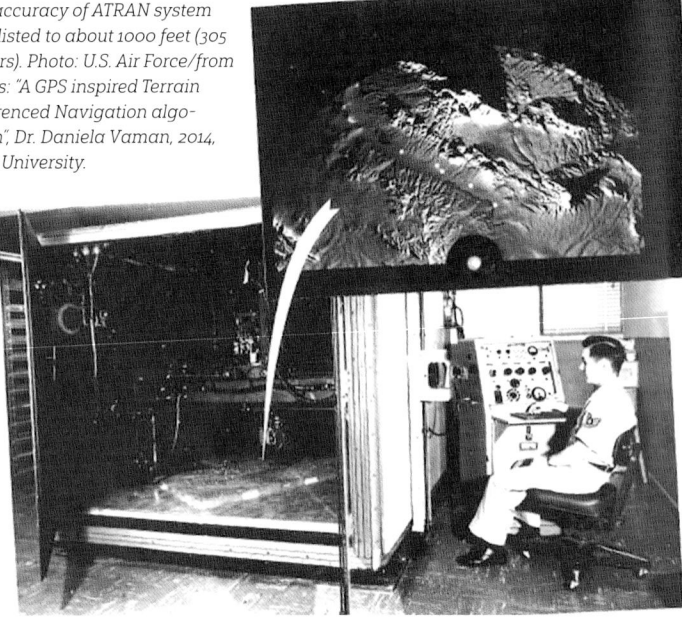

A distinct disadvantage of ATRAN was that it required extensive low-level aerial photography of each potential missile flight path. The danger to flight crews when flying over denied (USSR) territories made the system impractical. The U.S. Army Map Service created 3D relief models of the terrain of interest (painting known objects in white to produce strong radar reflections) and then made trajectory films by "flying" a motion picture camera over these models, as seen in these pictures. The accuracy of ATRAN system was listed to about 1000 feet (305 meters). Photo: U.S. Air Force/from thesis: "A GPS inspired Terrain Referenced Navigation algorithm", Dr. Daniela Vaman, 2014, Delft University.

Massive RB-50D in action

Much of the mapping was done by an improbable airplane that dated back to WWII. It probably created as much concern and surprise as any ever flown for low-level intelligence-gathering missions. Massive four-engined RB-50Ds, improved versions of the B-29 Superfortress that had carried the atomic bombs against Japan, were also used to collect critical mapping information in Germany in 1956 and 1957.

Flying the heavily modified RB-50D bombers out of Rhein-Main Air Base was the 7406th Support Squadron. Like the C-54D, the bombers were modified for their reconnaissance task by Goodyear and General Dynamics in Akron, Ohio, before being delivered to the 7406th in early 1956. The 7406th started flying the huge RB-50s on June 1, 1956.

The top-secret Half Track mapping mission supplied most of the actual flight maps for the new TM-76A Mace ATRAN map-matching guidance system. A typical mission consisted of a series of straight lines (tracks) from middle Germany to the East German border. It must have been a spectacular sight to witness a mighty RB-50 at low altitude roaring toward the border and then pulling up at the very last moment. There are tales of aircraft returning to Rhein-Main Air Base with tree limbs on the underside of the aircraft!

It was supposed to be a secret

While ATRAN was intended to be a super-secret missile guidance system—surrounding all activities in Germany, especially the ATRAN mission of the 7499th, with the utmost secrecy—in the U.S., the prime contractor Goodyear was apparently so pleased with the contract from the USAF that it began issuing press releases and publishing advertisements in the weekly Aviation Week

In the 1956 March 5th edition of the magazine it was revealed that a new, longer-bodied version of Martin's Matador ground-to-ground tactical missile had successfully completed a series of test firings at the Air Research and Development Command's Holloman Air Force Base.

It speculated that the new missile's longer nose section was probably meant for increased fuel capacity than that of the present Matador. The article stated that for tactical missions, it also would be equipped with an entirely new airborne guidance system. Another article appeared two months later.

In the May 7th edition of Aviation Week the new guidance system was announced. It was revealed that the new all-weather guidance system was called ATRAN and that it would be used in the Martin TM-61B Matador surface-to-surface missile, which was announced a couple of months earlier. Goodyear Aircraft Corp. had received a multi-million dollar contract for the system which was exclusively developed by them. ATRAN was housed in a self-contained nose package and required no external control from a "mother plane" or ground stations.

The Aviation Week article speculated that ATRAN may be an inertial or new type radar guidance system. According to the article, the test firings at Holloman AFB, N.M., were done using a modified TM-61A missile.

Goodyear publicly boasted ATRAN

Once again, Goodyear was extremely pleased with the contract they secured, to the extent that they proudly boasted about the ATRAN system in a double-page advertisement in the same May 7th edition of Aviation Week. They also introduced the concept of a "track" in collaboration with a four-engined aircraft and a fictional missile.

However, in reality, the ATRAN system proved inadequate in practice. While the analogy to railroad tracks was deliberately chosen, it ultimately compromised the Half Track project it referred to. Half Track now took on the meaning of "half of the job," specifically referring to the portion of the missile's trajectory over friendly territory and the educated guesswork for the segment over enemy territory, which neither Lulu Belle nor Half Track could accurately map, if at all.

New guidance system for TM-76B

The advent of the Cold War drove continuous development in radar technology, leading to advancements in detection, guidance, navi-

Goodyear's advertisement in Aviation Week stirred up some controversy within the USAF. It marked the first and only time that Goodyear openly published information about the ATRAN system, providing a rough explanation of its operation and inadvertently revealing part of the code name of the ATRAN mission in Germany. It is safe to assume that there were some heated discussions in Goodyear's offices following this incident. Subsequently, Goodyear advertised ATRAN only once more, and that too, merely as part of a list showcasing the company's innovations. Contrary to the belief expressed in several specialist publications, it appears that this publicity did not directly lead to the abrupt termination of the 7499th ATRAN mission. There was a significant gap of almost six months between the publication and the mission's termination. Additionally, the subpar quality of flight lines produced by Lulu Belle and Half Track likely played a role in their discontinuation. The decisive factor, however, was probably the introduction of the TM-76B, equipped with the state-of-the-art A.C. Spark Plug AChiever INS inertial guidance system. This system had remarkable capabilities, including a range six times greater than that of the TM-61A. The Matador had to be relocated significantly closer to the East German border for the USAF to target locations in the German Democratic Republic (GDR). With the MACE-B, which was not mobile, the 71st Tactical Missile Squadron at Bitburg Air Base could now reach targets in Poland and Czechoslovakia as well.

Chapter Two - **Dancing the corridors**

The cancellation of Lulu Belle and Half Track made the deployment of C-54 42-72684 from the 7405th SS and the RB-50Ds from the 7406th SS unnecessary. The C-54 was reassigned to other operational duties until its retirement from service in 1962. The RB-50s were promptly recalled to the U.S., marking the transition for the 7507th SS to contribute to the USAFE missile force.
Two B-57Bs from the 38th Bomb Wing in Laon, France, were allocated to the 7407th as part of Project Hygiene and converted to MSB-57B aircraft. Each of the two B-57s was equipped with an ATRAN nose radome, replacing the original noses, and used for testing the Shanicle guidance system. The MSB-57s, with serial numbers 52-1539 and 52-1562, were stationed at Sembach Air Base, where they became part of the 38th Tactical Missile Wing. This wing operated Mace A missiles from three remote sites: the 822nd TMS at Mehlingen, the 823rd TMS at Enkenbach (photo on the right), and the 887th TMS at Grünstadt.
Photo above: 887th TMS/ Fred Horky.
Photo below: 823rd TMS/Paul Monahan.

gation, telemetry, and remote control. It did not take long for a new guidance system to emerge for the TM-76B Mace B missile. This system was announced on September 24, 1956, as General Motors' A.C. Spark Plug Division's AChiever INS inertial guidance system. While it might seem unexpected that a spark plug factory would contribute to this innovation, it was, in fact, General Motors' electronics division, A.C., that provided the groundbreaking electronics for the Mace B. A.C. achieved considerable success and played a crucial role in the Apollo project during the 1960s. Notably, A.C. was responsible for guiding Apollo 11 into Moon orbit and providing navigation and fly-by-wire control for the Lunar Landing Module's descent to the surface. This achievement was the culmination of two decades of development.

The A.C. Spark Plug Division initially ventured into inertial guidance and navigation systems for the United States military in the late 1940s, starting with airplanes and jets, and later extending to missiles like the TM-76. They also contributed to the Titan III intercontinental ballistic missile, which was rumored to possess the ability to accurately target any window frame on any floor of the Kremlin, though the precise method remains classified. What is evident is that electronic navigation and guidance technology advanced rapidly in the latter half of the 1950s, rendering the ATRAN system obsolete. The introduction of the A.C. inertial guidance system and the advanced TM-76B led to the early discontinuation of both Lulu Belle and Half Track. Contrary to some publications, the cause does not seem to be compromising reporting in Aviation Week. The Aviation Week publication occurred in May, while Lulu Belle was halted in the fall of 1956, half a year later.

The actual reason likely lies in the low quality of the produced flight lines, coupled with the

30 Secret Mission

positive and thus jamable guidance control by radar-directed ground controllers, which limited the range. The TM-76B, in contrast, was a true fire-and-forget weapon capable of targeting its objective from a much greater range, making it suitable for deployment in Germany.

Carol Ann in disguise

Gradually, the older types where the 7405th SS was equipped with until then, were replaced by more modern equipment. In July 1958, the squadron's last RB-26 was retired, but there was also an influx of new equipment. A single C-118A (serial number 53-3278) was received that same month, and in January 1959, a C-54G (serial unknown) entered service. In September 1959, four CT-29As (series 49-1910, 49-1912, 49-1917, and 49-1933) were received to replace the old C-47s. The last Gooney Bird was transferred out in May 1960.

The 7405th SS had gained the additional task of providing courier services to Berlin for the U.S. military garrison in the city, and the T-29s were used as courier aircraft; they were known by the code name Carol Ann. Needless to say, these aircraft were equipped with various reconnaissance components that came in handy during daily service to Berlin. The C-118, which had been shot down in 1958, was replaced by a C-54, which was eventually retired in 1963. This plane was, in turn, replaced by two C-118s, which were mainly used for courier services to U.S. embassies in the Middle East. The squadron was retired from this type of mission on September 30, 1965, and the C-118s were reassigned.

Two types of C-97s

Two distinctively different C-97 sub-types were received in the early 1960s: three ELINT C-97s (often erroneously identified as "EC-97s"), used for electronic eavesdropping, and two photoreconnaissance C-97s (erroneously identified as "RC-97s").

The photo C-97s were real special birds; one of them (serial 52-2687) carried a 48-inch oblique-looking panoramic camera, a 12-inch vertical-looking panoramic camera, an infrared

scanner, a forward-looking infrared sensor (FLIR) and four electronic intercept stations.

The other (serial 52-2688) carried a 66-inch gyro-stabilized camera system, among others. The camera ports were hidden behind sliding external panels or in retractable domes. There were panels on both sides of the fuselage behind the forward entry door in front of the wing. Behind these doors were various sensors that required critical temperature stabilization before the mission. These had to be cold-soaked for several hours before takeoff. All mission equipment was hidden below the deck in the C-97. The planes could carry both actual cargo and unwitting passengers while collecting intelligence.

Two of the ELINT C-97s (serials 52-2639 and

The Convair CT-29s of the 7405th SS (Project Carol Ann) had a tri-metragon camera system in a covert compartment in the far aft section of the aircraft. This camera simultaneously provided coverage straight down and on the right and left side of the plane. Photo: Ralf Manteufel.

Boeing C-97A in Rivet Stem configuration comprised a 48-inch KA-81, a 12-inch Ka-82, and an RS-10 infrared camera. C-97 52-2687 remained with the 7405th SS until December 18, 1975. It was the last aircraft to depart from Wiesbaden Air Base where this photo was taken. Photo: Henk Scharringa.

Chapter Two - Dancing the corridors

C-97 navigator Don Backer:
"We took pictures the whole way in and out."

Only the 7405th aircraft conducted their own navigation over the corridors, following different routes, routinely deviating 500 feet (152 meters) from their assigned altitudes, and often flying random flight patterns. Both the Soviets and East Germans took pictures of the aircraft, clearly showing open camera doors. It must have appeared suspicious when as many as fifteen men disembarked from one of the planes, had lunch, then reboarded the aircraft and departed, all without transporting a single passenger or piece of cargo. This behavior led to the nickname "Berlin for Lunch Bunch." Years after the secret missions of the 7499th had ceased, it was revealed that MiG-19 and MiG-21 units based at the Soviet air base near Zerbst in the southern corridor knew precisely what the Americans were doing, despite all the security and secrecy. The Soviets used to fly high-level escorts in the corridors, hoping the Americans would make a mistake and veer out of the corridor, providing an opportunity for interception. The photo below vividly illustrates how narrow the approach to the runways at Tempelhof was. It attracted spectators, particularly on the Oderstrasse side of the runway, where the aircraft passed just a few hundred feet from the apartments on Leinestrasse. Photo: Ralf Manteufel.

During the daily missions to Berlin, pilots tried, when necessary, to fly as close to the edges of the flight corridors as they could get (they named it "The Corridor Dance), which enabled the photographers on board to reach as far as possible into Eastern Bloc territory. One of the best cameras available for the mission was a gyro-stabilized camera. Former squadron member and C-97 navigator Don Backer recalls these missions: "The cameras were run from hidden, claustrophobic compartments on the plane. When a target was in sight, we gave instructions to the pilot to allow the photographers the best access to the target."

Pushing the envelope

They constantly pushed the envelope when it came to staying in the corridor, and, as Don says, "We took pictures the whole way in and out." Once the plane arrived in Berlin, everyone debarked, had lunch, and then flew back to Wiesbaden. It was common for them to spot East Germans taking pictures of the unit's aircraft, the pilots, the crew, etc. Don said: "On one occasion, we flew at night using infrared night vision equipment. We were asked to make a swing over the recently opened new Soviet Embassy in East Berlin". The detour drew a lot of protesting over the airwaves, but we always were a little slow at following instructions, and the task was completed. Our intelligence agencies now knew which rooms in which buildings housed the communications and electronic equipment. The rest was up to them."

Only detected once

The only "detected" violation of Soviet airspace that he experienced, occurred when they were photographing a new Yak-28P. As Don recalls, "A special Soviet squadron of these new Firebars had been seen training at a large East German airfield just outside the southern corridor, and there was a high-level request to get shots of an open radome on the nose of the aircraft so that would enable analysts to determine frequencies and study the equipment. As we approached the target, we could see a maintenance stand and workers on the nose of a Firebar. I placed our best equipment on the target and coaxed the pilot closer and closer, getting pictures all the way. Multilingual hollering in our headsets prompted us to abruptly turn back toward the middle of the corridor as Soviet fighters approached from the rear. Our pilot apologized quickly and profusely for the dumb new man he was training and the compass that seemed to be broken".

Abstract from Joy Nelson's blog "The Berlin for Lunch Bunch", 2007.

52-2686) were equipped to fly peripheral missions only and never flew the Berlin corridors. They had multiple electronic warfare officer positions and sophisticated equipment on the cargo deck and also had a distinctive canoe-like dome under the fuselage. These aircraft frequently flew missions along the Iron Curtain and other target nations ranging from the Baltic to the Adriatic, Black, and Eastern Mediterranean Seas. They kept close track on the target nations' electronic systems, especially their air defense radar networks.

They operated along these routes from 1963 to about 1969-70, when their mission was taken over by Strategic Air Command (SAC) RC-135s. The third ELINT C-97 (serial 53-106) was equipped with specialized equipment designed to gather high-quality technical data on the Soviet SA-2 SAM (Surface-to-air Missile) system, which, by the mid-1960s, had spread throughout the Warsaw Pact countries, especially in East Germany, and was downing U.S. aircraft over North Vietnam.

While using the information gathered during these C-97 reconnaissance missions in the corridors, engineers designed active and passive electronic countermeasure systems against the SA-2. Both the north and south corridors were good places for this collection, as several Soviet SA-2 SAM sites were located directly within corridor limits. When the SA-2 was replaced by more advanced missile systems, the C-97 was modified to collect data on them as well.

The Dukes of Rhein-Main

In 1975, this C-97 was retired and the special technical ELINT collection package was transferred to one of the newer C-130Es. In December 1975, C-97G 52-2687 flew the last C-97 mission from Wiesbaden, and the 7405th, renamed the 7405th Operations Squadron on January 1 1973, moved to Rhein-Main Air Base. At that time, the unit had received the first of its three heavily modified Big Safari C-130Es to replace the C-97s. Much like their predecessors, these aircraft, operating under the code name Rivet Duke, were equipped with a variety of sensors boasting advanced capabilities. They carried five optical systems. Center piece was a one-and-a-half-ton KA-81 long-range oblique camera with a 48-inch (1,200 millimeters) focal length which could be electrically be repositioned to face either the left-hand or the right-hand side of the aircraft. This camera was covertly installed in standard C-130 cargo container and mounted in the cargo bay, directly behind the flightdeck. Two KA-82 panoramic vertical cameras were covertly installed under the cargo bay floor. An AAD-5 infrared linescan sensor for nighttime use or in restricted visibility, was concealed under the floor, with the sensors aligned with the leading edge of the wing root and the underside of the aircraft. In the rear of the left main undercarriages well was a SPF-1 FLIR (Forward-Looking Infrared) camera hidden, mounted in a retractable ball.

10,000 missions to Berlin

The corridor missions over the Berlin Air Corridors continued through the late 1980s. Then came the fall of the Berlin Wall in 1989, the subsequent reunification of Germany, and the withdrawal of Soviet forces from East Germany.

The final C-130 data-collecting mission was flown on September 27, 1990, and a week later, on October 3, the corridors ceased to exist. By that time, over 10,000 missions had been flown to Berlin. With the disappearance of the unit's "raison d'être," the 7405th SS was inactivated on March 31, 1991.

Lockheed C-130E Hercules aircraft from the 7405th Support Squadron were regular visitors to NATO air bases. Pictured here is C-130E 62-1828 in standard Europe One camouflage at Soesterberg Air Base, Netherlands. Externally, the C-130Es appear similar to any standard USAF C-130E, but what sets apart the Rivet Duke C-130Es is a third HF wire antenna extending from the tail to the fuselage—unlike the usual two antennas on a standard C-130E. The most significant differences, however, lie within the aircraft. During missions, special equipment operated through covert windows in the fuselage's side and belly. These windows remained hidden behind precisely machined pneumatic doors, capable of swift opening and closing within seconds. On 62-1828, as shown in the photograph, three circular portholes are visible in the forward fuselage. The middle one is deceptive—it is part of an 18 x 30-inch (46 x 76 centimeters) retractable door covering a 2-inch (5 centimeters) optical glass aperture. This setup allows the KA-81 to capture images from inside the pressurized cabin.
Photo: Jan van Waarde.

Chapter One - All-out intelligence

Aircraft known assigned to 7505th SS/OS

Serial number	Type/model	Description/background
42-72255	Douglas C-54D	Reportedly, 42-72667's serial was changed to "44-72255" sometime in late 1955. The actual 44-72255 was lost in a takeoff accident in England, on April 21, 1945. In any case, 42-72255 was active with the 7405th SS as an ELINT aircraft (as part of Project Pretty Girl) from late 1955 until February 1963, when it was Struck off Charge (SOC).
42-72465	Douglas C-54D	Previously with the 7499th SS, it remained under the 7405th SS until May 1964, when it was flown back to the USA and scrapped.
42-72502	Douglas C-54D	It was assigned to the 2058th Air Weather Wing at Wiesbaden in 1951 and moved to the 7405th SS in November 1957; no further details are known.
42-72667	Douglas C-54D	Previously with the 7499th SS, it was assigned to the 7405th SS on May 19, 1955. For reasons unknown, the aircraft received the fake serial 42-72255 in August 1955.
42-72685	Douglas C-54D	Converted for photo, infrared, and ATRAN work from June 1955 onwards as part of Project Lulu Belle and initially assigned to the 7499th Support Group in December 1955 but transferred to the 7405th SS in February 1956. It flew operational missions until it was returned to the USA in November 1962 and SOC in July 1964.
43-15221	Douglas C-47A	Previously with the 7499th SS and assigned to the 7405th on May 10, 1955. It remained active until at least September 1958.
43-17199	Douglas C-54D	Assigned to the 7405th SS in September 1957. It went to FAA in 1962 and registered N83.
43-17223	Douglas C-54D	Assigned to Twentieth Troop Carrier Squadron, it took part in the Berlin Airlift. It was with the 7405th in 1958. It went to Americade Corp. in September 1966, registred as N68783.
43-17248	Douglas C-54D	It was with the 7499th SS as part of Project Hot Pepper. Active until at least December 1958 and possibly as late as 1962, when it was transferred to the Pacific theater and reportedly received the fake serial "43-17235", which was from a C-54D that was damaged by a tornado March 20, 1948 after which SOC followed on May 8, 1948.
43-48186	Douglas VC-47D	Assigned to the 7405th SS for a brief period between June 1958 and August 1958.
43-49207	Douglas C-47D	With the 7405th SS between October 1956 and November 1958. To Portuguese Air Force as FAP 6164 in May 1961.
44-34416	Douglas RB-26B	Previously with the 7499th SS. It remained active with 7405 SS until at least July 1958.
44-34550	Douglas RB-26C	Previously with the 7499th SS, it remained active with the 7405 SS until at least July 1958.
44-35245	Douglas RB-26C	Active with the 7405th SS between December 1956 and December 1957 at least.
44-35343	Douglas RB-26C	Previously with the 7499th SS, it remained active with the 7405th SS until transferred out in June 1958.
44-35914	Douglas RB-26C	Previously with the 7499th SS, it remained active with 7405th SS until transferred out in July 1958.
49-1910	Convair T-29A	Assigned to the 7405th SS in March 1958. It was used as the unit's training aircraft and was redesignated CT-29A in July 1959. It was flown to Fort Worth, TX, on June 11, 1968, and was later reassigned to 6314th Strategic Wing (SW) at Osan Air Base, Japan.
49-1912	Convair T-29A	Assigned to the 7405th SS in January 1959. It was redesignated CT-29A in July 1959. It was flown to Fort Worth, TX, on June 11, 1968, and was later reassigned to 6314th SW at Osan Air Base, Japan.
49-1917	Convair T-29A	Assigned to the 740th SS in 1959. It was redesignated CT-29A in July 1959. On February 9, 1967, the aircraft crashed in a field near Breckenheim, about two miles northeast of Wiesbaden Air Base. On February 13, 1967, the aircraft was SOC at Wiesbaden and was put on the fire dump.
49-1933	Convair T-29A	Assigned to the 7405th SS in September 1959. It was redesignated CT-29A in July 1959. It was flown to Fort Worth, TX, on August 13, 1968, and was later reassigned to the 6314th SW at Osan Air Base, Japan.
49-2592	Boeing C-97A	Pie Face reconnaissance aircraft, previously with the 7499th SS. In 1957, the aircraft was painted as "49-2612" for a while but reverted to its original markings. That serial belonged to a C-47A that crashed in poor weather on a mission from Taegu to Kimpo, Korea, on May 26, 1951. Departed for USA on October 12, 1962, and flew missions around Cuba during the Cuban Missile Crisis. Scrapped in 1963.
51-0246	Boeing KC-97F	Flew with the 7405th SS between the fall of 1963 and 1964, acting as a C-97 crew trainer with no reconnaissance equipment. Returned to USA in 1964.

Serial number	Type/model	Description/background
51-3822	Douglas C-118A	CIA C-118 was attached to the 7405th SS in May 1955. It was shot down by MiG-17s on June 27, 1958, over Armenia and crashed in Azerbaijan.
51-3823	Douglas C-118A	Ex 1611th ATW and assigned to the 7405th SS on July 24, 1963. It received the bogus serial number "13842" in July 1965. It was transferred to the 1405th AMAW at Scott AFB, departing on October 5, 1965, where it received its original serial number again.
51-3825	Douglas C-118A	Ex 1611th ATW, assigned to the 7405th SS on July 24, 1963. It received the bogus serial number "13846" in June 1965 and was transferred to the 1405th AMAW at Scott AFB, departing on October 5, 1965, where it received its original serial number again.
53-3278	Douglas C-118A	Ex 1611th ATW, assigned to the 7405 SS on July 17, 1958. It was reassigned to the 1100th ABW at Bolling AFB, departed on January 19, 1960.
52-2639	Boeing C-97G	Conversion to reconnaissance standard started in March 1962. Assigned to the 7405th SS in spring 1963. Modified as ELINT aircraft in Project Little Guy and became Rivet Gumbo in early 1966. Transferred back to USA in September 1970, sold to Israel.
52-2678	Boeing C-97G	Assigned to the 740th5 SS in fall 1967. It was not a reconnaissance aircraft but was used as a crew trainer and support aircraft. Returned to the USA in November 1969.
52-2686	Boeing C-97G	Conversion under Project Speed Light Alfa to ELINT aircraft started in July 1961, but this was changed to Project Small Fry in November 1961. Assigned to 7405th SS by autumn 1964. Returned to the USA in December 1969. Transferred to "another agency" on May 2, 1971.
52-2687	Boeing C-97G	It was a combined ELINT and photoreconnaissance bird; conversion to this configuration started under Project Flint Stone in July 1961. Assigned to the 7405th SS in July 1963 for operation in the Berlin Corridors. The project name was changed to Rivet Stem in 1969. Returned to USA in December 1975.
52-2688	Boeing C-97G	Conversion to photoreconnaissance aircraft under Project Eager Beaver started in July 1961, and delivery to the 7405th SS was in July 1963. The project name changed to Rivet Box in January 1967. The C-97 remained active until February 1970, when it went back to the USA.
52-2724	Boeing C-97G	It was converted to photoreconnaissance aircraft under Project Rivet Giant and served in the Pacific before being assigned to the 7405th SS in the early 1970s.
53-0106	Boeing C-97G	A Greek Flie ELINT aircraft that was assigned to the 7405th SS in the spring of 1964. Part of a CIA-directed program to collect data on SA-2 missiles, flew the Berlin corridors, passing over SA-2 sites. Modified for Project Wine Sap ELINT missions in 1965. The project name was changed again to Rivet Stock on November 16, 1967. Remained active until 1975, when it returned to the USA.
53-306	Boeing C-97G	Converted to photoreconnaissance configuration as Project Cindy Fay which was later changed to Rivet Flare. Served in the Pacific before being assigned to the 7405th SS in September 1970. Active until at least 1973.
62-1819	Lockheed C-130E	Previously with the 37th TAS/316th TAW (coded 'LM'), it was delivered to the 7405 OS in March 1976 under the Big Safari program Rivet Duke. Departed to the USA in December 1990.
62-1822	Lockheed C-130E	Previously with the 316th TAW (no code), it was delivered to the 7405th OS in December 1975 under the Big Safari program Rivet Duke. Departed for the USA for rework early in 1990.
62-1828	Lockheed C-130E	Previously with the 37th TAS/316th TAW (coded "LM"), it was delivered to 7405 SS in October 1975 under the Big Safari program Rivet Duke. Departed for USA again in December 1990.

Lineage 7405th Support/Operations Squadron

Established under 7499th Support group in May 1955 based at Wiesdbaden. Moved to Rhein-Main and redesignated 7405th Operations Squadron in December 1975. Assigned to the 7575th Operations Group in July 1977. Last corridor flight September 27, 1990. Inactivated January 1991.

Attached aircraft

Since the 7499th, the CIA has made grateful use of the facilities provided, such as maintenance and daily support. A variety of espionage aircraft were used over the years. Remarkably, many types were given bogus serial numbers. CIA planes at Wiesbaden include (with the real identity in brackets):

- C-54D 43-17206 (U.S. Navy as BuNo 56533)
- C-54D 43-17216 (mystery plane)
- C-54D 43-17236 (U.S. Navy as BuN 56538)
- C-47A 44-77036 (RAF Dakota IV KN665)
- C-54G 45-533 (mystery plane)
- L-20A 51-6266, 51-6267, 51, 16269, 51-16465
- L-28A two unidentified planes, possibly 58-7026/7027
- RB-69A (P2V-7U) 54-4038, 54-4039 (tests only) 54-4040, 54-4041
- U-2A/B (Det. A) 56-6679/80/81/84 (Article 346/347/348/349)

Lockheed C-130A-II 56-0530 on the taxiway at Rhein-Main in 1970. There were few features to distinguish the aircraft from normal cargo C-130s, apart from the lack of camouflage and the presence of the enlarged pods under each wing, which contained some of the aircraft's sensors and equipment. Photo: Peter Zastrow.

Chapter Three

The eavesdroppers

Wiesbaden developed into the intelligence center of the U.S. government at the end of World War II. It is also home to the headquarters of the Bundesnachrichtendienst (BND), the German intelligence agency, making the capital of the German state of Hesse the El Dorado of secret services. Not far to the east is Frankfurt, which has evolved into a European financial center.

Frankfurt is also the seat of the largest U.S. consulate in the world and serves as a diplomatic hub globally. The U.S. diplomatic center in Frankfurt oversees embassies and consulates in 140 countries. Additionally, as the consulate functions as a training and management center, there is significant diplomatic air traffic at the U.S. air base Rhein-Main near Frankfurt, known as the Gateway to Europe by the Americans. Unlike Wiesbaden-Erbenheim Air Base, now called Lucius D. Clay Kaserne after General Lucius D. Clay, the American military commander during the Allied occupation of Germany after World War II and mastermind of the Berlin airlift Operation Vittles in 1948, Rhein-Main had the capacity for many large aircraft.

The base boasted two parallel runways of 7,000 and 6,000 feet (2,133 and 1,828 meters) and an extensive tarmac area. Therefore, it was a strategic decision by the 7499th Support Group to station the 7406th and 7407th Support Squadrons there instead of Wiesbaden.

Airborne reconnaissance

Like the other units, the 7406th SS was formed following the reorganization of the 7499th SS on May 10, 1955. The new squadron had a very modest start, consisting only of one officer, the commanding officer, Capt. William P. Fisher, and a single airman upon activation. On June 17, the first shipment of office supplies arrived, and the squadron headquarters operations were set up at Rhein-Main, which would serve as the home base for almost two decades.

The primary mission of the 7406th was airborne reconnaissance, carried out by the RB-50E and RB-50G versions of the bomber. Both were modified RB-50Bs, featuring a capsule in the rear fuselage carrying nine cameras in four stations and the capability to carry 700-US-gallon (2,650 liter) drop tanks under each outer wing. The E-version was designed for photoreconnaissance and specialized observation on long-endurance missions, upgraded with an in-flight refueling system. It retained the standard defensive armament of thirteen .50-cal. machine guns, with major updates to reconnaissance photo equipment and the relocation of camera platforms for increased stabilization needed for new higher resolution cameras. The RB-50E usually had a crew of ten. The G-version was fitted with a SHORAN radar for short-range precision navigation and six electronic stations. The electric spyplane required a crew of sixteen.

Meanwhile, an influx of personnel arrived at Rhein-Main, many of whom were trained on B-50s from the 98th Bombardment Wing, deployed to RAF Lakenheath in England at the time. By June 1956, over one year after its activation, the unit consisted of 29 officers and 86 airmen. They were ready to operate with the RB-50D, although only one RB-50 was available at that time. That was 48-0107, which landed at Rhein-Main as early as March 6, 1956

Challenging start

Upon arrival at Rhein-Main, all aircraft still carried different designations (B-50D, JB-50E, and EB-50D), but on October 1, 1956, all three aircraft were officially redesignated Boeing RB-50D. Under the code name Half Track they formed Flight A, specializing in ATRAN low-level operations in support of the Matador cruise missiles stationed at Bitburg and Hahn Air Bases. However, the use of the ATRAN-project Lulu Belle Douglas C-54 by the 7405th was not overly successful, and with the 7406th, the RB-50D also proved troublesome.

The unit had a challenging start due to technical problems during the modification process at Goodyear in Akron, Ohio, causing the delivery of the three aircraft (serial numbers 48-0107, 49-0307, and 49-0312) to be delayed until the spring of 1956. To compound the issue, upon arrival at Rhein-Main, it was discovered that 49-0312 was in such poor condition that the unit immediately grounded it and cannibalized the aircraft for parts for the other two. After extensive efforts by the 7406th maintenance unit during a four-month restoration, it returned to flying status at the beginning of 1957.

By June 1, 1956, the first operational ATRAN low-level missions were flown by the two op-

In December 1955, B-50D 49-0307 was converted to RB-50D under Project Half Track and delivered to the 7406th Support Squadron in May 1956. In 1951, this Boeing was part of the FICON (Fighter Conveyor) program conducted by the United States Air Force in the early 1950s to test the feasibility of parasite fighters. The B-50 was equipped with a cable and winch to test the feasibility of towing a fighter. The tests were conducted at Edwards Air Force Base in April and March 1951, towing a Lockheed T-33A (49-0938) during eleven successful trials. RB-50D 49-0307 soldiered on after the ATRAN project was halted in October 1956. It became a trainer aircraft until it returned to the USA in August 1958 to become a TB-50D used for crew training.

Chapter Three - **The eavesdroppers**

The Dream Boat missions were conducted using Boeing RB-50E/Gs, typically flying at 24,000 feet (7.315 meters), with a duration of no less than 12-14 hours. As depicted on the map, RB-50s operated from their home base, Rhein-Main, as well as forward bases, covering various corners of Europe. During these missions, they followed hour-long COMINT tracks along the borders and coasts of the Soviet Union.

Post-1966, the 7406th Support Squadron transitioned to conducting all C-130A/B-II COMINT missions under the code name Creek Grass. These missions mirrored those of the RB-50, and operations expanded to include North Africa, the Eastern Mediterranean, and the Caspian Sea. C-130A-II missions were flown at 28,000 feet (8,534 meters) with durations ranging between seven and nine hours.

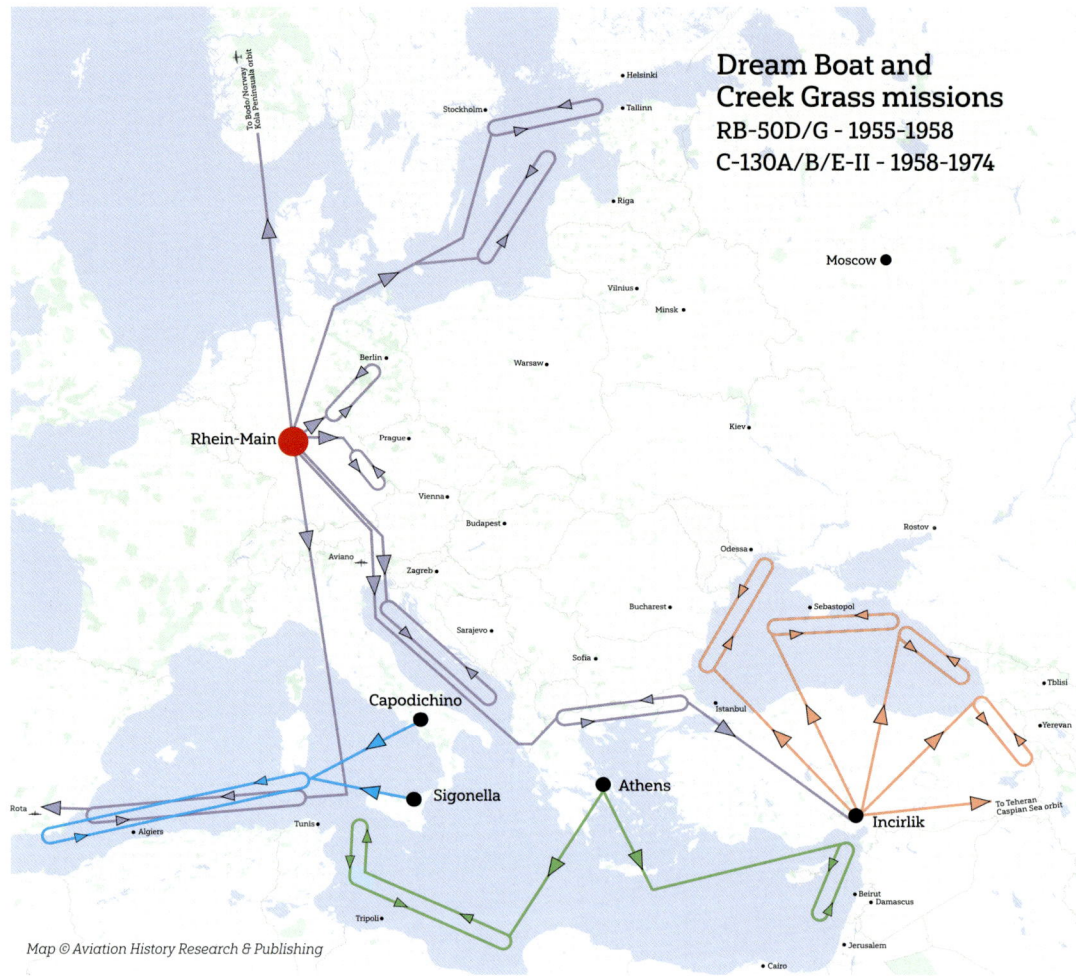

Map © Aviation History Research & Publishing

erational RB-50s. The RB-50 crew would fly as straight a line as possible from the middle of Germany to the East/West German border at altitudes between 500 and 1000 feet (152 and 304 meters) and pull steeply up at the border. The two-man ATRAN operators sat on a platform in the forward bomb bay and collected radar imagery of the terrain.

Initially, about seven Half Track missions were flown weekly. When the ATRAN missions were halted on October 19 due to the disappointing results, 52 missions were completed. The Half Track program was officially terminated in January 1957, and the 7406th could start focusing on other intelligence duties. One of the Half Track RB-50Ds (serial number 49-0307) continued with the unit and served as a temporary trainer aircraft. For that purpose, it was stripped of its armament and the external fuel tanks. Eventually, the plane returned to the USA in August 1958.

Paint it black

The squadron's main mission was COMINT, communications intelligence, which is the interception and analysis of radio communications. Under the code name Dream Boat, eavesdrop missions were flown along Europe's eastern borders and coasts. Five aircraft formed Flight B of the 7406th: three RB-50Es (serial numbers 47-120/126/129) and two RB-50Gs (serials numbers 49-136/157). The aircraft were delivered between 1956 and 1958. The RB-50s retained the defensive armament consisting of four remotely controlled turrets and a manned tail gun position. They also had additional radar equipment.

Secret Mission

Although they had been delivered in a natural metal finish, the bottoms of four of the RB-50s were soon painted flat black, while the natural metal on the rest of the fuselage was retained. However, one aircraft, 47-0157, was painted all black. This black paint was not the most durable ever applied, and the aircraft quickly gained a very mottled appearance.

Five Russian linguists/radio operators were an important part of the crew; they occupied two positions immediately aft of the navigator's position. There was also a single radio technician who had to look after the equipment while airborne. The operators monitored radio traffic overheard during the mission and recorded everything for subsequent interpretation.

Missions of twelve to fourteen hours

In December 1956, Flight B commenced long-range navigation training flights using the former Half Track RB-50s. On January 12, 1957, the first operational Dream Boat mission was flown with 47-0157; at that time, the unit's only available COMINT aircraft.

The missions usually lasted twelve to fourteen hours and were flown at 24,000 feet *(7.315 meters)* altitude. Some missions were more common than others, and the most regularly ones followed six different routes. One was from Rhein-Main to the Baltic Sea. They would fly north, up the middle of the Baltic Sea east of Gotland to a point east of Stockholm, and then start an orbit between Sweden and Finland and return. The other concerned a relatively short triangular track over Germany. A longer flight was from Rhein-Main, along the Balkans, to the Adriatic Sea en route to Adana, Turkey (Incirlik Air Base) and return to Rhein-Main. When, in early March 1957, a permanent detachment was formed at Incirlik, there were orbit missions flown from Incirlik along the Black Sea coast and missions from Adana to Trabzon and Lake Van.

The Norwegian air base Bodo was designated the 7406th Support Squadron's Det #2 and from there RB-50s flew missions along the Soviet coast of Murmansk on the Kola Peninsula. This detachment continued operations until 1964, but no aircraft were ever permanently stationed there. Apart from the above, during the years of operations, missions were also flown over the Eastern Mediterranean (especially during the various Arab-Israeli crises) and anywhere else they were urgently needed.

After 1966, the COMINT missions of the 7406th continued under the code name Creek Grass which were flown with Lockheed C-130A/B-IIs.

A mechanic's nightmare

It turned out that the RB-50 was the mechanic's nightmare; the troublesome Pratt & Whitney R-4360 engines were notorious. These 28-cylinder, four-row air-cooled, radial engine produced 4,300 hp (3,200 kW) and tended to

Two Boeing RB-50Gs were in service with the 7406th Support Squadron. They were from a series of five B-50Bs (47-133/136/149/151/157) that had been converted to RB-50Gs suitable for ELINT operations in 1950. By 1955, under a program called Haystack at Texas Engineering and Manufacturing Company (Temco) at Majors Field in Greenville, Texas, the aircraft had been converted primarily for COMINT operations. Also under the Haystack program were five RB-50Es (47-120/124/126/127/129), which had previously been converted for special photographic missions. The Haystack RB-50Gs retained their armament and were partly painted black. The aircraft's finish suffered considerably from the heavy use; the paint peeled off, and the engines, in particular, needed a lot of maintenance. RB-50Es 47-120/126/129 and RB-50Gs 49-136/157 were operating with the 7405th, the other Haystack aircraft went to the 6091st Reconnaissance Squadron at Yokota Air Base, Japan.

Michel Debarre

Chapter Three - The eavesdroppers

RB-50 pilot Albert S. O'Connor:

"Our .50-inch kept the Soviet jets away."

Albert O'Connor, son of the late Maj Albert S. O'Connor Sr (USAF, Ret.), passed on a few of his father's stories for this book which give an insight of the hazards encountered in the early days.

" According to my father, back then in the 1950s, the USAF used ground-based navigation beacons to determine their distance from the Soviet-Armenian airspace/border. They flew close to Soviet airspace. My father did not talk much about the hardships he endured flying these ELINT missions, but they lived in tents out in extreme elements, flew from ramshackle airstrips but later on they flew from paved runways and had buildings to live in, but that was after he left that Area of Operations.

Close encounter at Lake Van

My father said he remembered one particular mission where he flew his RB-50G to Lake Van to begin his racetrack orbit along the border. In the RB-50G, they shut down two of the four engines and feather the props as to save fuel and extend their time on station, so the technicians in the back could do their eavesdropping and monitoring of Soviet military communications. During this particular mission, the Soviets "lit up" his plane with ground-based radars and his techs told him that the Soviets had scrambled a flight of MiGs and had directed the jet fighters to the B-50's location. It was common knowledge that the Soviets consistently and constantly ignored national borders and they would routinely cross into Turkey, to harass or try to shoot down these unarmed ELINT planes.

My father said he didn't sit around waiting for the MiGs to show up, because all he had available to him in the RB-50G were two .50 caliber machine guns in the tail of the plane. He started the two feathered engines he had previously shut down, went to full military power, to the firewall, and dove the plane down to the deck so he could "hide" his plane from the high-flying Russian MiGs and also "disappear" from their ground based radar in ground clutter and any possible aerial radar the MiGs may have had. Flying the huge lumbering RB-50G on the deck enabled him to get himself and his crew to safety on many an occasion.

What is ironic is that the RB-50G had no paint on it (it still carried silver aluminum color) with international red paint on the wings, vertical and horizontal stabilizers. So "hiding" while flying on the deck was a bit of a joke, that plane stuck out like a sore thumb if seen from above (this was the reason black paint was later applied – author). He also said that during another flight he was shadowed by MiGs and saw tracers fly ahead of his plane's flight path but his plane was never actually attacked directly. He said he felt the twin .50s helped keep the jets, in that particular incident, at standoff range."

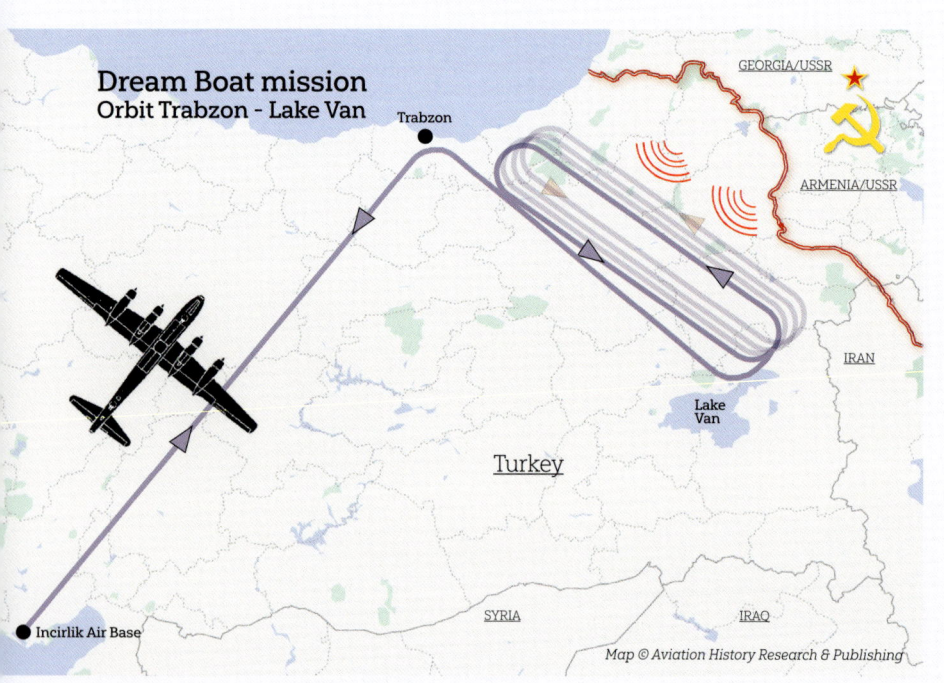

40 Secret Mission

overheat during high-altitude missions. It was not unheard of to shut down one or two engines and restart them again after they had cooled down a bit. One crew member remembers: "The temperature in the aircraft was quite difficult to control. If you went from the front of the aircraft to the rear, you had to go through a 25 feet tunnel over the bomb bays, and sometimes, the front of the aircraft was cold and the aft was 85°F (29°C). Things broke down: we frequently came back on three engines, or with the radar out."

The arrival of the C-130

Although the B-50s had been in use for only a very short time, a replacement was on the way, and in May 1957, the squadron was told they would receive specially modified Lockheed C-130 Hercules planes in 1958 instead of C-118s, which were initially planned to be the replacements for the RB-50s (the RB-50 was considered to have been a stopgap solution pending the arrival of the C-118). The first Hercules, C-130A-II with serial number 56-0484, was delivered in June 1958. The new C-130s were specialized for COMINT collection. This was a highly classified mission at the time, and it still is, over sixty years later. The C-130 pilot training was done at Évreux-Fauville Air Base in France, a regular USAFE C-130 transport base and home of the 322nd Air Division that directed all airlift units assigned to USAFE. As soon as sufficient C-130 aircraft had been received, the last RB-50s were retired, or rather, they were reassigned to the 6091th Reconnaissance Squadron (RS) at Yokota Air Base, Japan, in October 1958. During the changeover of aircraft types, the detachment at Bodo, Norway, was retained, and in August 1958, the first C-130-A-II (serial number 56-528) flew to Bodo on a training mission. The U.S. high command had requested the Norwegian government to allow missions out of Bodo to within 100 miles off the coast of Russia. The Norwegians, however, denied the permanent stationing of American spy planes on their territory.

A sad chapter

The year 1958 marked a sad chapter for the 7499th. First, a C-118 deviated from its course en route to Tehran and was lost over the Soviet Union. Then, on September 2, tragedy struck again, this time with fatal consequences for the crew. The squadron lost C-130A-II with serial

Lockheed C-130A 56-0535 was converted to a C-130A-II Dream Boat electronic surveillance configuration by the Texas Engineering & Manufacturing Company (TEMCO) under Project Sun Valley. It was flown by two pilots with a navigator and radar navigator, a flight engineer, and scanner. There were ten radio operators and a radio repair technician. The cargo compartment had been converted to three radio compartments. The two forward compartments each had voice intercept positions for four operators, while the third had only two. A galley and radio repair station were at the rear. Radio antennas were installed in fiberglass pods resembling fuel tanks. In the aircraft's nose was the AN/APN-59 navigation, search, and weather radar. The C-130A was equipped with four Allison T56-A-9 turboprop engines, driving three-bladed propellers.
Photo: Peter Zastow.

Chapter Three - The eavesdroppers

(201) Am climbing, climbing.
(582) I can see the target on the right.
(582) I can see the target, it is a large one.
(201) I can see the target!
(...) What sort of target is it?
(...) The target is a large one.
(218) Am attacking.
(582) Didn't hit.
(201) Am attacking the target
(...) I've hit it, I've hit it, I've hit it!
(201) Am attacking the target.
(...) Hurry up 201.
(...) The target's speed is 300. I am along side it. It's turning towards the frontier.
(582) Look the target is burning! It's been hit.
(...) The target is banking.
(...) It's going towards the frontier.
(...) No.3 open fire!
(201) 218 are you attacking?
(218) Now, I am yes!
(...) The tail unit has broken away from the target.
(582) Watch where it is going.
(...) He isn't getting away. He is already falling. Force him down to the west! Force him straight down!
(...) The target is out of control, it's going down. The target has turned over. The target is falling.
(...) All the aircrew are on board, aren't they?
(...) Yes, form up and go home.
(...) after my first burst the target caught fire, and then everybody hit it in turn.
(582) No... nobody jumped.

Extract from the translation of the Soviet VHF voice traffic during the attack on September 2, 1958. Source: National Security Agency.

number 56-0528 following an attack Soviet MiG-17s. The C-130 was on a reconnaissance mission along the Turkish/Armenian border when it wandered into Soviet airspace. Apparently, there was no intention for the aircraft to actually fly over Soviet territory.

Lured into Soviet airspace?

All seventeen crew members on board perished in the crash near the village of Sasnashen, 34 miles (55 kilometers) northwest of Yerevan, the Armenian capital; six members from the 7406th and eleven from the 6911th Radio Group (Mobile) at Darmstadt. The aircraft was flying a mission out of Incirlik on the Mediterranean coast and was due to fly from there to Trabzon on the Black Sea coast, turn right, and fly to Lake Van, Turkey, where an orbit was started between Van and Trabzon, gathering data all the time. Although the course of this orbit paralleled the Soviet border, the aircraft would never be closer than about 100 miles (161 kilometers). During the final orbit, the crew reported passing over Trabzon at an altitude of 25,500 feet (7,772 meters) and acknowledged a weather report from Trabzon – and the aircraft was never heard of again. According to Major Albert S. O'Connor Sr. (USAF, Ret.), a former B-50 and C-130 pilot with the unit, the crew was lured into Soviet airspace by Soviet navigational beacons in Armenia and Soviet Georgia, which were on frequencies similar to those at Trabzon and Van. However, post-Cold War studies have found no evidence for that theory, and there is some evidence to support multiple navigation errors; the definitive cause remains unclear.

Anyway, at 3:04 p.m., the aircraft crossed into Soviet airspace. Soviet air defense radars had been tracking the aircraft for some time and one flight of two Mikoyan-Gurevich MiG-17 Fresco interceptors from the 25th Fighter Regiment from Yerevan were scrambled to intercept the C-130. The weather was good, with visibility of 9-12 miles (15-20 kilometers). The first flight of MiGs was commanded by Senior Lieutenant V.V. Lopatkov (582). His wingman was Senior Lieutenant H. Govrilov (583). According to a COMINT report from the National Security Agency (NSA) which was declassified in 2009, there was a second interception flight that scrambled from Leninakan (now known as Gyumri). Leninakan was home of the 117th Fighter Regiment that operated the MiG-17 interceptors. The commander of this second flight was Senior Lieutenant Kucheryaev (201), his wingman was Senior Lieutenant Ivanov (218).

Going down on fire

The first flight intercepted the C-130 at approximately 3:08 p.m., and Lopatkov reported firing warning shots at 3:09 p.m. The C-130 started to maneuver and tried to limb away and escape to the Turkish/Armenian frontier. The Soviet pilots asked for and received their command post's permission to engage the C-130 and commenced the attack at 3:12 p.m.

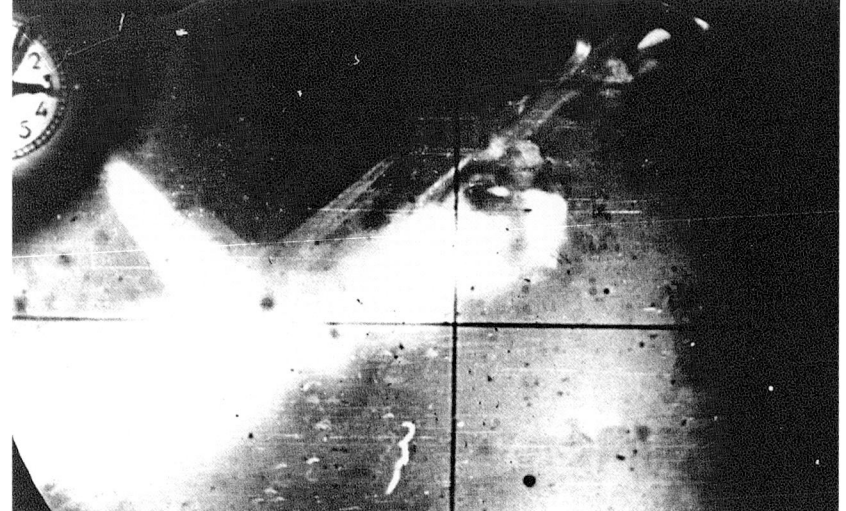

42 Secret Mission

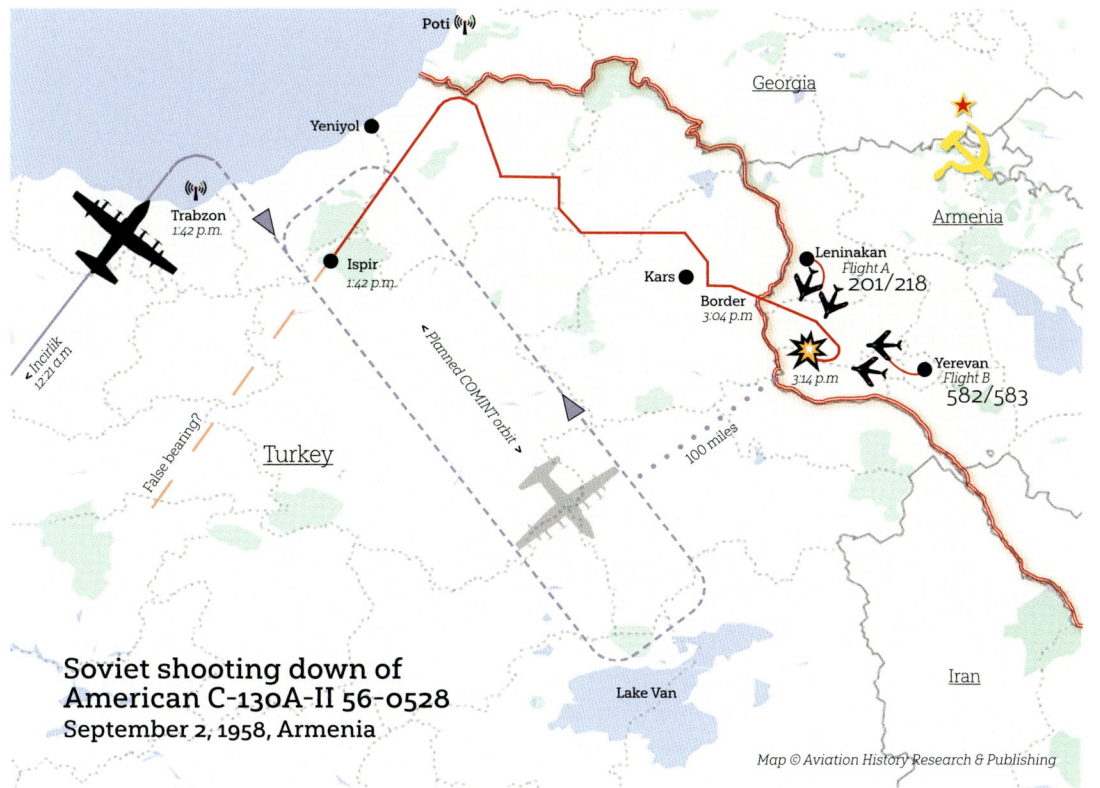

Soviet shooting down of American C-130A-II 56-0528
September 2, 1958, Armenia

Map © Aviation History Research & Publishing

After the Cold War, the Soviet Union released several documents detailing the last flight of C-130 56-0528. The map and the information below are based on the document "Shooting down of the U.S. C-130 transport aircraft in the Transcaucasus" released by the National Security Agency on August 31, 2009. The flight plan of C-130A-II 56-0528 was Adana (Incirlik)-Trabzon-Lake Van-Trabzon-Adana. The aircraft took off from Incirlik at 1:21 p.m., and at 2:42 p.m., the navigator reported its position as "over Trabzon." After 2:42 p.m., no further positions were received from the aircraft. The Soviet Air Warning Organization had started to track the flight at 2:41 p.m., and at 2:42 p.m., the Soviets plotted its position to the vicinity of Ispir, some 80 miles east of Trabzon. According to the Soviet tracking radar, it continued to a position slightly east of Yeniyol. Right at the frontier, it turned to the southeast towards Kars. East of the city of Kars, the C-130 turned east towards the frontier, which was crossed at 3:04 p.m. Two MiG-17s (582 and 583) had already been scrambled from Yerevan. Five minutes later, the C-130 was intercepted by MiG-17 582, and at 3:12 p.m., the American intruder, flying at an altitude of 32,800 feet (10,000 meters), was attacked by MiG-17 201. In the following minutes, all four MiGs fired at the C-130, which went down at 3:14 p.m. near the village of Sasnashen.

Below: Mikoyan-Gurevich MiG-17 Fresco "201" from the 117th Fighter Regiment at Leninakan.

All four Soviet aircraft attacked the aircraft, disabling at least one of the C-130 engines and setting it on fire. The pilot of the fourth MiG reported that the C-130 was going down on fire and was shedding parts even before he began his attack, although it remained largely intact until it crashed. Following the incident, the Soviets denied downing the aircraft, claiming that the C-130 "fell" on their territory.

On September 24, 1958, the Soviets returned six sets of human remains but, when queried, stated they had no information regarding the eleven missing crew members. Although the U.S. State Department released an authentic audio tape of the Russian pilot's conversations, the Soviets described the recording as "fake." They continued to deny responsibility for the downing, and the fate of the remaining crew members remained unknown until the end of the Cold War, when some of details of this shooting down emerged.

As they did with the B-50s, the unit flew missions with the C-130s along the edges of the Eastern Bloc countries, from the Baltic Sea

Michel Debarre

Aviation History Research & Publishing

Chapter Three - The eavesdroppers

C-130A-II 56-0525 during takeoff. Note the grey finish and the very plain markings. Externally, the C-130A-IIs looked like ordinary Hercules transport planes, except for the large pods on each outer wing. These pods looked like fuel tanks, but the fiberglass pods housed UHF/VHF radio antennas. Photo: Via Henk Scharringa.

all the way to the Caspian Sea. The C-130s made long hours and expanded on the number of missions flown by the B-50s in previous years.

The Creek Grass missions by the C-130A-IIs were flown at 28,000 feet (8,534 meters) and typically lasted eight hours and forty minutes, but continuously added equipment led to a weight increase, and by 1970, mission duration was down to seven hours and thirty minutes. The original mission times were restored to the old level with the introduction of the C-130B-II in 1971.

An odd duck in the crowd

An interesting sideline is the short-time use of a former U.S. Army De Havilland C-7B Caribou (serial number 61-2600). It was initially used as a aft by the 507th USASA Group (U.S. Army Security Agency), but when the USAF gained control over the former Army C-7Bs (or CV-2As as they called them) on December 31, 1966, the role was transferred to 7406th SS as Project Creek Moose.

A separate flight was formed within the unit to operate the aircraft, which was flown and maintained by USAF personnel, but the operators in the back were U.S. Army personnel, who lived in the same barracks as the USAF squadron members. Army maintenance procedures differed from those in the USAF, and the aircraft had several inspections due when it was received in February 1969. Upon completion of these, the Army demanded a receipt and received standard USAF laundry receipt, which they accepted..! Operational C-7B SIGINT missions started in January 1970 and usually lasted three hours, taking them all along the Iron Curtain. On July 31, 1970, the aircraft was reassigned to the 516th TAW at Dyess Air Force Base, Texas, ending the Caribou operations for the unit.

Baltic Sea reconnaissance

Some of the typical missions flown included those from Rhein-Main to the Baltic Sea, where they orbited off Gotland, off the east coast of Sweden. This was a challenging environment: in the 1960s, Soviet Mikoyan-Gurevich MiG-17PF Fresco interceptors were based in

A one-off aircraft used by the 7406th was C-7B 61-2600, which was delivered to the unit in 1969. Partially crewed by U.S. Army operators in the cargo hold, it was involved in SIGINT missions, flying missions along the Iron Curtain. The photograph was taken at Rhein-Main on May 23, 1970, by Lindsay Peacock.

Secret Mission

Latvia, and Mikoyan-Gurevich MiG-19 Farmers and Yakovlev Yak-28P Firebars flew out of Kaliningrad; these fighters regularly intercepted the C-130s. In addition, on June 16, 1967, a C-130 experienced an unintentional near miss with a Soviet Air Force Antonov An-12 over the Baltic! These Baltic Sea missions ended in June 1973, when jet-propulsed Boeing RC-135 Stratolifters from the 55th Strategic Reconnaissance Wing (SRW) replaced the C-130s.

More benign missions were flown over central West Germany, orbiting along the Czech and East German border. The detachment at Incirlik (also known by the crews as "Inkydink"!) was still active as well. The squadron deployed aircraft there for longer periods, usually two weeks at a time, and during such a TDY (Temporary Duty), several missions were launched from Incirlik and recovered there again. On the way back home to Germany, tvhe C-130s would usually be stocked with things like oranges, grapefruits, nuts, and leather goods, which were hard to get by in Germany.

Black Sea reconnaissance

Apart from Turkey, all countries bordering the Black Sea were of interest to the squadron, especially Sevastopol, the large Soviet naval base in Crimea. From May 1963, the Detachment at Incirlik would also send aircraft to Tehran's Mehrabad Airport, Iran, for short detachments to fly missions over the Caspian Sea. The Iranian heat presented the crews with some unique problems: when temperatures were over 95°F (35°C) inside the aircraft, the mission equipment did not work properly, so to reduce the cabin heat some tasks started with the aircraft's top hatches open. However, in December 1965, a Martin/General Dynamics RB-57F Canberra of sister squadron 7407th SS crashed in the Black Sea, and this caused such a diplomatic upheaval that from that date onwards, all missions over the Black Sea and the Caspian Sea were suspended.

From 1966 to 1974 (with a short break in April 1967 and early 1968 due to Greek reluctance to allow these flights to be flown from their territory), the unit also had a detachment at Hellenikon Air Station, just south of Athens, Greece, from where missions could be flown over the eastern Mediterranean, along the coast with Syria, Lebanon, Israel, and Egypt, with the occasional orbit at the request of the intelligence crews in the back.

This area was especially important during the Israeli-Arab wars in 1967, 1970, and 1973, when the unit received help from the Navy, who were flying Lockheed EC-121Ms, EP-3Bs, and EP-3Es on similar missions. From August 1, 1968, the Greek detachment was known as Det 3. The unit's area of operations was not confined to those mentioned above.

The C-130B-IIs carried camouflage, unlike the C-130A-IIs. Compared to the "normal" C-130B, these reconnaissance aircraft sported a few additional antennas, as well as the pod under the wing. In several publications these C-130s have been referred to as RC-130Bs, but actually the correct designation is C-130B-II; this designation was also used by the unit itself. The aircraft at right is 59-1530 on October 20, 1972, seen taxiing past the well-known spotters spot "Zeppelinheim" next to the A-5 Bundesautobahn. Photo: Peter Zastow.

Chapter Three - The eavesdroppers

All over the world

A near-permanent detachment was established at MacDill Air Force Base, Florida, which operated from 1964 until 1971, with at least one aircraft present in Florida at any given time. From MacDill, missions were flown along the northern coast of Cuba; the unit often worked in coordination with Lockheed U-2s during these missions, listening in on Cuban responses in reaction to a U-2 overflight.

The unit also operated from the other side of the world; on February 19, 1967, two aircraft, 56-0534 and 56-0541 and four crews, departed for a period of TDY at Yokota Air Base in Japan, for Operation Creek Mark to assist the Airborne Communication Reconnaissance Program (ACRP) mission there. The 556th Reconnaissance Squadron, based at Yokota Air Base, Japan, flew the C-130B-II, mostly over Korea, the South China Sea, the Gulf of Tonkin, and Vietnam. The 7406th C-130A-IIs flew local missions out of Yokota over the Sea of Japan, relieving the C-130B-IIs to fly missions in Southeast Asia. The aircraft returned to Rhein-Main in June 1967.

In July 1971, news was received that the squadron's A-models were to be replaced by the C-130B-II. Crews went to C-130 school at Little Rock AFB, A.R., and indeed, on October 16, 1971, the squadron received the first of five C-130B-IIs. A month later, the unit was assigned to the 322nd Tactical Airlift Wing at Rhein-Main and redesignated Operations Squadron. The old A-models were all reconverted to "trash haulers" and assigned to Air National Guard (ANG) units.

SAC takes over

Because of the increased tension in the Middle East, the squadron's operations from Hellenikon, Greece, gained importance. The location was of strategic importance because from here the C-130s could easily reach the coasts of North Africa and the East Mediterranean. By the end of 1971, over fifty percent of the missions were flown from here. At one point, all available flight crews were sent to Athens due to increased mission requirements, and by June 1973, following the cessation of the Baltic missions, all operational missions were flown out of Athens.

By then, the squadron's mission requirements had been substantially reduced, and several aircraft were reassigned to Air Force Reserve (AFRES) units in the U.S. By 1974, the squadron was no longer needed, and the Mediterranean mission was taken over by SAC RC-135s of the 55th SRW, which also maintained a detachment at Hellenikon. Actually, the final C-130B-II mission was flown on June 14, 1974, and the last four aircraft departed Rhein-Main for the USA on June 26 that year.

A job well done

A few days later, on June 30, the 7406th Support Squadron was inactivated; the official ceremony was held two days earlier, attended by the USAFE brass band and the commander of 17th AF, Major-General John Giraudo. During that ceremony, a message from General David C. Jones, Commander-in-chief of USAFE, was read to the squadron. It concluded: "The sincere dedication and professionalism displayed by your personnel in performing their mission in support of national tasking is recognized not only in USAFE but by the highest national authority. Many thanks for a job well done."

*The 7406th flew all its operational missions out of Hellenikon from July 1, 1973, until its last C-130B-II mission was flown on June 13, 1974. After the inactivation of the 7406th OS on June 30, 1974, the unit's mission was taken over by the 55th Strategic Reconnaissance Wing (SAC) based at Offutt AFB, Nebraska. This unit operated Boeing RC-135 aircraft, which were regularly deployed to European bases like Mildenhall, Hellenikon, Souda Bay (Crete), and Incirlik. Below Boeing RC-135V 64-14848 Rivet Joint with its distictive Side Looking Airborne Radars (SLAR) showing an arsenal of ventral and dorsal antennas.
Photo: Cees Steijger/AHR&P.*

Aircraft known assigned to 7506th SS/OS

Serial number	Type/model	Description/background
47-0120	Boeing RB-50E	Ex 6091st RS, delivered to the 7406th SS on January 7, 1958. Returned to the USA on October 27, 1958, for further modification work and reassigned to 6091st RS at Yokota, Japan.
47-0126	Boeing RB-50E	Ex 6091st RS, delivered to the 7406th SS on February 28, 1957. Returned to the USA in July 1958 for modifications and reassigned to 6091 RS at Yokota, Japan.
47-0136	Boeing RB-50E	Ex 6091st RS, delivered to the 7406th SS on October 5, 1957. Returned to the USA on October 2, 1958 for further modification work and reassigned to 6091st RS at Yokota, Japan.
47-0157	Boeing RB-50G	Ex 4024th BS/97th BW at Biggs AFB underwent modification work at Oklahoma City (Air Logistics Complex) ALC and with TEMCO at Greenville in 1956 before being delivered to the 7406th SS on March 17, 1957. Returned to the USA on April 12, 1958, for further modification work and reassigned to the 6091st RS at Yokota, Japan.
48-0107	Boeing RB-50G	Spent time with Oklahoma City ALC and Goodyear at Akron for modification work in 1955 and 1956 before being delivered to the 7406th SS on March 5, 1956. It was redesignated as an RB-50D on October 1, 1956. Returned to the USA in January 1957, and eventually became a KB-50 tanker.
49-0307	Boeing JN-50D	Spent time with Oklahoma City ALC and Goodyear at Akron for modification work in 1955 and 1956 before being delivered to the 7406th SS on March 5, 1956. It was redesignated as an RB-50D on October 1, 1956. Returned to the USA in January 1957, and eventually became a KB-50 tanker.
49-0312	Boeing EB-50D	Spent time with Oklahoma City ALC and Goodyear at Akron for modification work in 1955 and 1956 before being delivered to the 7406th SS on April 3, 1956. It was redesignated RB-50D on October 1, 1956. Returned to the USA in February 1957, and became a test aircraft (designated JTB-50D) at Wright-Patterson AFB.
54-1637	Lockheed C-130A	To the 7406th SS in the 1960s. It departed in January 1972.
56-0484	Lockheed C-130A-II	To the 7406th SS in June 1958. It departed in April 1972 and was reconverted to C-130A standard.
56-0525	Lockheed C-130A-II	To the 7406th SS in July 1958. It departed in September 1972 and was reconverted to C-130A standard.
56-0528	Lockheed C-130A-II	To the 7406th SS in July 1958. It was shot down over Armenia on September 2, 1958.
56-0530	Lockheed C-130A-II	To the 7406th SS in October 1958. It departed in April 1972 and was reconverted to C-130A standard.
56-0534	Lockheed C-130A-II	To the 7406th SS in August 1958. It departed in December 1971 and was reconverted to C-130A standard.
56-0535	Lockheed C-130A-II	To the 7406 SS on July 4, 1960. It departed in December 1971 and reconverted to C-130A standard.
56-0537	Lockheed C-130A-II	Was with 7406th SS during the 1960s – no further details known.
56-0538	Lockheed C-130A-II	To the 7406th SS in January 1959. It departed in February 1972 and reconverted to C-130A standard.
56-0540	Lockheed C-130A-II	To the 7406th SS in October 1958. It departed in February 1972 and reconverted to C-130A standard
56-0541	Lockheed C-130A-II	To the 7406th SS in November 1958. It departed in January 1972 and reconverted to C-130A standard
56-0711	Lockheed C-130B-II	From the 556th RS to the 7406th SS on October 16, 1971, (still carrying the code "GT" from its former unit). It departed 1972 and reconverted to C-130B standard.
59-1524	Lockheed C-130B-II	From the 556th RS, to the 7406th OS in December 1971. It departed on June 26, 1974, reconverted to C-130B standard.
59-1526	Lockheed C-130B-II	From the 556th RS to the 7406th OS by March 1973. It departed by 1974 and reconverted to C-130B standard.
59-1527	Lockheed C-130B-II	From the 556th RS to the 7406th OS in January 1972. It departed (date unknown) and reconverted to C-130B standard.
59-1528	Lockheed C-130B-II	From the 556th RS to the 7406th OS on November 27, 1971. It departed (date unknown) and reconverted to C-130B standard.
59-1530	Lockheed C-130B-II	From the 556th RS to the 7406th OS on January 1, 1972. It departed by 1974 and reconverted to C-130B standard.
59-1531	Lockheed C-130B-II	From the 556th RS to the 7406th OS in June 1972. Departed by 1974 and reconverted to C-130B standard.
59-1532	Lockheed C-130B-II	From the 556th RS to the 7406th OS in May 1972. Departed on June 26, 1974, and erconverted C-130B standard.
59-1533	Lockheed C-130B-II	From the 556th RS to the 7406th OS in April 1972. Departed 1974 and reconverted to C-130B standard.
59-1535	Lockheed C-130B-II	From the 556th RS to the 7406th OS on January 1, 1972, (still carrying the "GT" code from its former unit). Departed on June 26, 1974, and reconverted to C-130B standard.
59-1537	Lockheed C-130B-II	From the 556th to the 7406th OS on November 27, 1971. Departed by 1974 and reconverted to C-130B standard.

Lineage 7406th Support/Operations Squadron

Established under 7499th Support group in May 1955 based at Rhein-Main.
Assigned to 322nd Tactical Airlift Wing on November 15, 1971.
Redesignated Operations Squadron on November 15, 1971.
Opertions moved to Hellenikon, Athens, by June 1973.
Inactivated in June 30, 1974.

*In this photograph, RF-100A 53-1554 is captured in flight over Germany. This Super Sabre was one of the three Slick Chicks deployed to the 7407th Support Squadron. While flying over USSR territory, the RF-100As were required to use their afterburners to stay away from intercepting MiG 17s.
Photo: North American Aviation.*

Chapter Four

Behind the curtain

The third squadron that was activated on May 10, 1955, was the 7407th Support Squadron; it was stationed at Rhein-Main Air Base and also operated a detachment at Bitburg Air Base. Instead of lumbering propeller aircraft, the squadron was in the jet business.

High flying Canberras

The main body of the unit, at Rhein-Main, operated the Martin B-57 Canberra, and various models were used over the years. The squadron's first RB-57A (serial number 52-1492) also referred to as RB-57-0, had received special modifications for high-level oblique photography as part of Project Sharp Cut. The aircraft was delivered in the latter half of May 1955. It was fitted with a more compact version of the huge 240-inch camera mounted in the Pie Face C-97, and began flying peripheral clear sky missions exploring the camera's capabilities.

The rest of the squadron's RB-57As, six in all, arrived together at Rhein-Main, via Robins AFB, Goose Bay, and Keflavik, on August 23, 1955. These aircraft also had special modifications for Project Heart Throb, and were tasked with vertical photography. Unlike the Sharp Cut RB-57A, these were equipped for single-pilot operation, with the navigator's seat removed, and also lacked the armor and rotating bomb door and associated hydraulics of other B-57s. This weight reduction program was initiated to increase the aircraft's operational ceiling to 65,000 feet (19,812 meters). They were sometimes referred to as RB-57A-1s. The official squadron records, however, do not refer to these -0 and -1 designations. In October, one of the RB-57As was sent to RAF Burtonwood in the UK, where the underside of the aircraft was resprayed in blue-grey, in an attempt to improve the camouflage of the aircraft. However, it turned out that the new camo made the aircraft more visible when viewed from below and the aircraft was resprayed gloss-black again.

The squadron started training for the upcoming mission, with 7407th pilots reporting to two other other B-57 units of the USAF: the 38th Bomb Wing at Laon in France (a nuclear bombardment unit) and the 66th Tactical Reconnaissance Wing at Sembach, Germany (which had unmodified RB-57As assigned).

Between October and December 1955, the squadron was involved in exercise Red Fox, in which USAFE F-86s tried to intercept the high-flying B-57s. A few "normal" B-57s had accidents following problems with the B-57 variable-incidence stabilizer actuator, and this caused the grounding of the type within USAF twice in January and February 1956, followed by another 75-day grounding from May 1956. However, the 7407th SS was allowed to continue to fly due to the unit's vital importance. Although it was not their main mission, the Heart Throb project participated in various recconnaissance programs in Western Europe, including one to document the construction of U.S. bases in Spain in 1957, using the Heart Throb B-57s. Every now and then, a B-57 would head that way, fly a predetermined route, and return with the photographs.

Flying over communist territory

The main purpose of the Heart Throb RB-57As was to fly reconnaissance over communist territory (denied territory). President Eisenhower had reluctantly approved several Air Force military overflight programs because of the lack of knowledge about Soviet and satellite military capabilities. One of these programs was Heart Throb. From starting operations in September 1955 until November 1956, when the last overflight mission was flown, the 7407th flew at least nineteen overflight missions from Rhein-Main.

1956 was a volatile year, with the Suez Crisis and the uprising in Hungary. These overflight missions were carefully planned, and a number of predetermined desirable targets along the route were photographed. The 900 nautical mile mission radius of action of these special RB-57As, flying at about 60,000 feet (18,288 meters), enabled them to cover (weather permitting) virtually all the satellite nations from Poland through Hungary, as

A RB-57A in 1956 on the platform of the 66th TRW at Sembach Air Base, Germany. The aircraft has serial 52-1426 and is painted in a high-gloss black anti-searchlight livery, similar the Heart Throb RB-57As of the 7507th at Rhein-Main, Germany. Photo: U.S. Air Force. The photograph below captures a moment from the late 1950s, showcasing the simultaneous engine start-up of four RB-57As from the 7407th SS on the ramp of Rhein-Main Air Base. The smoke seen in the image arises from the cartridges used to initiate the engines. On the left, enveloped in smoke, is the squadron's sole T-33A. In the background are two C-124s. On the right, you can observe the B-29s 44-27295 and 44-86443, both former atomic bombers from the 509th Bombardment Group (Heavy). Photo: Via Henk Scharringa.

Chapter Four - **Behind the curtain**

RF-100 pilot Colonel Cecil Rigsby:
"I never felt threatened."

Colonel Cecil Rigsby, a former pilot with the unit, has some recollections of his time with the RF-100A: "In Germany there were no restrictions on supersonic flights; you could go supersonic at high or low altitude." The pilots started looking for the best possible flight profiles to attain the best performance in their F-100s. During a briefing at Wiesbaden, the men were told to perform the mission with the greatest secrecy, to make up a cover story and to tell no one, not even their wives, of the mission at hand.

Advantage over the MiG

There were some concerns over the outcome of an encounter with Soviet MiG-17s, as the F-100, without using afterburner to conserve fuel during a long mission, only had the slightest speed advantage over the MiG. "We made a lot of flights with clean configuration (no external tanks) to see how we might evade an interception. This is when the countryside, and our home base, experienced a lot of sonic booms. Those F-86 pilots were really jealous!"

After a period of training, the Det's RF-100As made at least six actual overflights over communist territory. From Bitburg, the RF-100, could cover most of East Germany and western Czechoslovakia. From Fürstenfeldbruck they could also cover western Hungary and northwest Yugoslavia. At least one of the operational missions, which originated from Fürstenfeldbruck, took the F-100 over Hungary and Czechoslovakia, including overflights of Bratislava and Prague. The mission's primary objectives were to obtain imagery of military airfields.

Once across the border, the F-100s would accelerate to Mach .95 or .96 in full military power. Col. Rigsby remembers one such flight: "As I approached the targets I began to see a flurry of aircraft activity. With my vertical cameras operating over one of the airfields, I could see through the viewfinder that there were several fighters taking off and several airborne. When I reversed my direction to return and had covered all my assigned targets, I had a lot of company on my departure. The fighters were going all out, but to match my speed they had to stay at a lower altitude, about 20,000 feet below me. They broke off when I reached the border and I recovered safely at Bitburg." Another mission took the RF-100A over East Germany; during this mission, the F-100s again encountered several enemy fighters, but Rigby confides: "I never felt threatened." One of the data interpreters, Major Roger Rhodarmer, recalls some details of the information gathered: "It was not the photography that was such a shock. When they did the first penetration, wherever it was they went, they encountered ten times more radars than we ever thought existed. They picked them up easily and tracked them easily every step of the way. Back in Washington with the Chiefs of Staff, everybody was shaken up to know that Soviet radars were thát good."

**Slick Chick
Eastern Block overflights**
Bitburg/Fürstenfeldbruck 1955-1956

Map © Aviation History Research & Publishing

Source: Symposium Proceedings "Early Cold War overflights 1950 -1956", Volume 1, February 22-23, 2001, Defense Intelligence Agency, Washington D.C.

well as parts of Yugoslavia, providing coverage that was unprecedented and extremely valuable.

The B-57s are known to have flown over cities like Budapest, Brno, Belgrade, Zagreb, and Bratislava, where airports, infrastructure, and industrial complexes were photographed. Most, if not all, missions were challenged by the countries the aircraft flew over, but although MiGs were invariably scrambled, they never succeeded in intercepting the high-flying B-57s.

At the start of a mission, the B-57 would always be accompanied by another aircraft that looked for the tell-tale contrails. If contrails appeared at the desired altitude, the mission would be aborted.

A formation of the three RF-100As of Detachment 1, 7407th Support Squadron at Bitburg Air Base, Germany. From left to right: 53-1545; 53-1551 and 53-1554. Photo: North American Aviation.

Slick Chick

In the meantime, an entirely different outfit had been set up at Bitburg. As part of 7407th SS the secretative Det 1 was formed there. It operated a special RF-100A recce variant of the Super Sabre which had been developed under the code name Project Slick Chick which aim was supersonic overflights of communist territory. The aircraft record cards initially referred to the aircraft as plain F-100As rather than RF-100As, although unit histories and other official records note them as RF-100As. It was thought that the sheer speed and agility of these modern fighters were sufficient to defeat Soviet air defenses. Six conversions were completed; three were assigned to 7407th SS and the other three to the 6008th Composite Group at Yokota in Japan. These aircraft, drawn from an early FY1953 production batch, were the first USAF F-100s to be based in Europe. Actually, they were the first supersonic fighters based in Europe. The RF-100As were considered to be an interim solution, pending the availability of the U-2. Development of the RF-100A had begun in 1953. They were equipped with five cameras using various focal lengths. An optical viewfinder was also fitted to the aircraft, as well as extended wing tips to enable the aircraft to reach 53,000 feet (15,240 meters), its intended service ceiling. Furthermore, all unnecessary equipment had been removed; this included the cannon and other weapon-related instruments. To house the cameras, a special camera bay was added to the aircraft's belly (see the photograph on page 52 and the profile below) which clearly distinguished the

On October 1, 1956, RF-100A 53-1551 crashed near Neidenbach, ten miles (16 kilometers) north of Bitburg Air Base. Capt. Ed Hill, piloting the Super Sabre, experienced an engine flameout at high altitude. Despite his efforts to relight the engine, Capt. Hill was unsuccessful. Faced with the situation, he opted to bail out rather than attempting a dead-stick landing

Chapter Four - Behind the curtain

Above, an RF-100A on the platform of the North American plant in Inglewood, California. The nose armament was completely removed and replaced by five reconnaissance camera systems that looked ahead and to each side of the aircraft. A distinctive bulge had to be added onto the fuselage belly underneath the cockpit to accommodate all of this equipment. This bulge extended from below the windshield almost to the wing trailing edge and was an obvious recognition feature. The RF-100As carried four drop tanks rather than the usual two, because the mission profile called for a lot of high-speed flight under afterburner, and there was no provision for midair refueling. A typical mission profile was to climb to an altitude of 40,000 to 43,000 feet (12,192 to 13,106 meters) approaching the Iron Curtain. When crossing the border, the pilot would select afterburner and climb to 50,000 feet (15,240 meters). Flying with full military power and afterburner at that altitude, the airplane would reach speeds of Mach 0.95 to 0.96. With this profile and using the afterburner, the range of the airplane was limited to 625 nautical miles (1,157 kilometers) with a fuel reserve of 500 pounds. Photo: North American Aviation.

type from the regular Super Sabre.

They were to be based at Bitburg, because Wiesbaden and Rhein-Main were considered to be unsuitable for fast-jet operations due to their insufficient runway lengths. Col. Cecil H. Rigsby would become the program leader in Germany. He was sent to Belfast early in May 1955 to oversee the arrival of the RF-100As by ship, they had just completed the Atlantic crossing from Mobile, A.L., on board the USS Tripoli. "We were all shocked to find that Belfast in May was the coldest place on earth. There was a constant 20 mph wind blowing across the city. To make things worse, the British do not believe in heating their buildings after April 30, no matter how cold it gets. There was only one good hotel in town and it was full. We got rooms in a hotel three stories high, made entirely of wood and about 100 years old. My face was a mess because my hand shook so much when I shaved in the morning."

Top secret outfit

All three F-100s eventually checked out OK and they departed Belfast for Bitburg on May 16, with a stopover at RAF Burtonwood. At Bitburg, the squadron's hardstands and newly erected hangar (which could only house a single F-100) were located in an isolated area between two of the based squadrons, with armed guards looking over the area 24/7 – this was a top secret outfit! Detachment strength was minimal at 36 officers and men. Flight training started on June 1, 1955. Co-located 36th FBW still flew F-86s, but was slated to receive F-100s in 1956, so all the pilots were very anxious to learn as much as they could about the new aircraft until they were officially told to stop asking questions!"

As was the case with the Heart Throb RB-57As, the Slick Chick RF-100As were never given another overflight mission after mid-1956. The reason was that President Eisenhower had approved the use of the new CIA-operated U-2As for overflight missions, and had ordered the Air Force to cease their own overflight program. In 1956, the first U-2 had arrived in West Germany and had begun flying operational missions in June. Det 1, however, remained fully combat ready.

One RF-100A, 53-1551, was lost in an operational accident in October 1956; it was later replaced by a brand-new standard F-100C (55-2711, formerly with 36th FBW) which was used as a training aircraft. There were a few other incidents like engine failures, but a particularly memorable one was the release of a drag chute while fling in afterburner at 50,000 feet (15,240 meter). Luckily, the afterburner flame burned it off before it could have any adverse effects. In May 1956, the 7407th had received a T-33A, serial number 51-6909, which was shared between Rhein-Main and Det 1 at Bitburg. It was used for aircrew proficiency training.

Finally, Det 1 at Bitburg ceased operations in the summer of 1958 and was officially inactivated on July 1, 1958. The RF-100As were flown to the storage depot at Châteauroux Air Base, France. In June 1959, they were shipped back to the USA, where the aircraft were modified and transferred to the Republic of China Air Force on Formosa (Taiwan) later that year.

Testing radars

In the meantime, the 7407th's connection with the B-57 continued when the first (52-1437) of two highly modified RB-57A-2s (which appears to be an unofficial designation as well) arrived at

Rhein-Main on August 8, 1957. These aircraft were equipped with AN/APS-60 mapping radar to test the operational capabilities and limitations of this radar, in a program known as Project "SARTAC." The meaning of this acronym remains unclear. The program was finished in June 1958 and the two RB-57As were ferried back to the USA that month, to be replaced by two B-57Bs (52-1565 and 53-3860). These aircraft were involved in a program named Project Hygiene and had ATRAN guidance systems installed which allowed them to simulate TM-61 Matador missile flight profiles (see Chapters Two and Three). One of the B-57s was fitted with the Shanicle (ATRAN) guidance system, and the other with the positive ground control (MSQ-1) guidance system, simulating both systems in use on the missiles. They were stationed at Rhein-Main, but often flew missions from Sembach AB, which was the home of the 38th TMW, which was the unit using the Matador missiles.

Until they were transferred back to the U.S. in 1960, they flew over 200 missions, testing the systems and simulating missile launches. They often deployed to Wheelus Air Base, Libya, where the missile crews conducted actual launches. In the fall of 1958 they worked out of Wheelus as part of Operation Marblehead, a large-scale exercise involving all of the missile wing squadrons.

High flying RB-57Ds

From 1958 to 1960, 7407th SS also used the two B-57Bs for transition training for the unit's RB-57Ds; they were also used to ferry high-priority cargo and regularly made trips to Incirlik Air Base in Turkey. In the late 1950s, bases like Incirlik, as well as Wheelus in Libya, and Moron in Spain were favorite destinations to escape the inclement German winter weather and to be able to continue training.

From January 1960, Nouasseur Air Base, French Morocco, became the unit's regular winter training site. During this first TDY in Morocco, Capt. Louis K. Godman became the first squadron pilot to suffer a double engine failure; he managed to land his powerless RB-57D safely at Agadir Air Base. In the spring of 1959, three pilots were sent to Laughlin Air Force Base, Texas, to start transition training on the RB-57D.

On June 9, six RB-57Ds (with the three "old hands" and three new pilots) were delivered to Rhein-Main Air Base. One of these six aircraft (63-3963) was of the RB-57D-1 variant, a single-seater equipped with a SLAR radar along the fuselage and a larger nose radome that was used for day and night radar mapping operations.

Other special features of this variant were an autopilot and folding rudder pedals; the latter allowed the pilot to stretch his legs during long flights. The other five were basic RB-57D-2s, all of them capable of in-flight refueling capability. These aircraft were two-seaters, with an enlarged nose to house a radar and a camera bay in front of the nose wheel well. Compared to the standard B-57B, the wing span had increased from 64 to 106 feet (19,5 to 32 meters). The RB-57Ds carried a distinctive color scheme, the fins and underside of the fuselage being black, and the upper surfaces retained the natural metal finish. They were assigned to the Big Safari program and replaced the older Heart Throb RB-57As, which were all transferred to 154th TRS, Arkansas ANG.

This RB-57D (serial number 53-3974) was code named Black Knight 3 and operated under the secret Big Safari program. It was one of the thirteen single seat photoreconnaissance RB-57Ds. All RB-57D operations of the 7407th were under heavy security and very little information has been released about their operations in Europe. They presumably carried out a variety of intelligence missions along the East German border and over the Baltic Sea.

Chapter Four - Behind the curtain

The squadron also "owned" this Martin TB-57C, 53-3857, which replaced the Lockheed T-33A, 51-6909, as their crew trainer. Nicknamed Porky, it served with the unit between 1959 and 1968, and is seen here at Rhein-Main in plain markings on May 18, 1968. It returned to the USA just three months later, on August 27, 1968, and joined the 58th WRS at Kirtland AFB.
Photo: Jack Friell via Steve Miller.

RB-57D, serial number 53-3972 somewhere over the USA prior to assignment to Rhein-Main. Originally, it was a single-seat Canberra, but a second crew position was added to operate the mission equipment.
Photo: U.S. Air Force.

At the same time as the RB-57Ds, a single TB-57C (53-3857) was delivered for crew training. This aircraft replaced the T-33A. As the squadron's old RB-57As had been used as crew trainers as well, the squadron received a B-57E to replace them on October 14, 1960, and following removal of the target-towing equipment, the aircraft was referred to as a TB-57E in official squadron papers, but not on official USAF record cards. Finally, on November 30, 1960, the squadron's last RB-57A, 52-1492, was flown back to the USA. Although some have assumed that the RB-57D missions included incursions into Eastern Bloc airspace (including missions over Hungary), none did in fact take place, and overflights had officially been terminated following the U-2 downing in 1960. However, the aircraft did fly many missions along the IronCurtain, photographing everything with their powerful on-board cameras.

Almost straight up

There was some light-hearted inter-squadron rivalry as well. Former 7407th member Herb Greathouse recalls the following incident: "During the 1961 Rhein-Main air show, there was a standard cargo C-130 aircraft doing a demo short field takeoff. This was a scheduled display item for the air show that day. After the C-130 did its demo, one of our pilots went to our secured area unannounced. He took one of our RB-57Ds to show off the airplane, called the control tower on the radio and asked for permission to do an "Unscheduled" demo takeoff. He received permission and outdid the C-130, using less runway to get airborne, climbing almost straight up, then spiraling back down, landing in front of the crowd and taxiing back to our secure area. The entire squadron was loudly cheering him on! The guys that flew these planes were a class of their own." Herb also remembers that: "Being stationed in Germany in the '60s was fun, just plain fun, and at four Deutschmarks to the U.S. dollar your money went a long way."

Fatigue cracks

An interesting operation was Project White Christmas, which brought RB-57D-1 53-3963 to Thule Air Base, Greenland, for a few weeks in late November and early December 1960. The aircraft was used to determine whether or not high-resolution radar could be used to detect objects under ice and snow. In late 1960/early 1961, the squadron sent its RB-57Ds back to the U.S., where they were extensively modified at. The first one, 53-3975, left on July 7, 1960, and received major modifications at the Fort Worth facility of General Dynamics. The mods took place under the Big Safari project called Paper Doll and included the installation of the "Big Item," an oblique camera installation centered around a camera with a 240-inch (6,000 mm) lens. Designated as Black Knight 1, 53-3975 was reassigned to the 7407th on

The impressive wing of 63-13500 is the most distinctive feature of the RB-57F. Other noticeable changes include the use of different engines; Pratt & Whitney TF33 turbofans. For a comparison, please refer to the other B-57 photographs on previous pages. Also note the podded engines just outside of the nacelles.
The photo left of 62-13500 during final approach to Rhein-Main was shot by Manfred Faber.
The photo below was shot on July 13, 1966, by Paul Bennett (via Glynn Evans).

March 22, 1961. It remained in service until June 9, 1962, when fatigue cracks were discovered in the front wing spar, prompting the grounding of the aircraft. The RB-57D's large wing design posed additional challenges. The non-fatal crash of NRB-57D 53-3973 ('N' for Special Test) in the USA on January 4, 1964, was attributed to problems with the wing's structure. This incident led to the immediate grounding of the entire RB-57D fleet, including the examples in the 7407th SS.

By then, the squadron was already slated to receive the RB-57F, but this was still some way in the future. Only three of the unit's five RB-57Ds were in such a condition that they were cleared to fly back to the USA, the last two leaving together on March 16, 1964. The other pair was airlifted back to the USA; the last of these left on May 20, 1964. For the next year or so, the squadron only had the TB-57C and B-57E assigned. The latter was transferred out in August 1965.

The RB-57D's replacement was the RB-57F, and the first of these for the 7407th SS was 63-13500, which arrived at Rhein-Main AB on April 4, 1965. The second RB-57F, 63-13287, was delivered to the unit on October 29. These aircraft had some extraordinary high-altitude capabilities, but ranked high amongst the most ungainly looking aircraft ever built! It was almost impossible to see the family resemblance with the original Canberra; it featured a larger tail, different fuselage, Pratt & Whitney TF33 turbofan engines and optional extra Pratt & Whitney J60 podded turbojet engines, which boosted the ceiling of the RB-57F over a stunning 80,000 feet (24,384 meters). The booster jets could be removed and replaced by sensor pods or fuel tanks to increase the plane's range. But what distinguished the RB-57 the most were its huge wings, with a wingspan of just over 122 feet (37 meters). They made the plane very challenging to land because it tended to stay in the air due to the significant ground effect. The RB-57F was able to carry the two-ton so-called HTAC high-altitude reconnaissance camera which could take pictures from 60 miles (97 kilometers) away, and ELINT/SIGINT equipment was carried in the nose and wingtips.

Chapter Four - Behind the curtain

On the night of December 14, 1965, a Martin RB-57F Canberra, piloted by Capt. Lester Lackey with 1st Lt. Robert Yates as navigator, was last reported approximately 90 miles (145 kilometers) north of Turkey over the Black Sea. Initial beliefs pointed to the possibility of the aircraft being struck by a Soviet SA-2 missile, resulting in a crash. Subsequent investigations, however, suggested that the crash occurred due to a loss of oxygen and subsequent loss of consciousness. Capt. Lackey and Lt. Yates were listed as Missing in Action (MIA). Although debris from the downed aircraft was discovered in the Black Sea near Turkey, no bodies were ever found.

A terrible accident

However, on December 14, 1965, all went terribly wrong during a mission along the Black Sea coast. RB-57F 63-13287 had been at Incirlik Air Base, Turkey, since November 23, and had been flying operational reconnaissance missions. The aircraft crashed in the Black Sea during one of those missions (although USAF reports at the time quoted that the aircraft was on "a routine training mission"), causing considerable political upheaval between the USA and Russia.

Salvage operations were difficult and both sides tried to recover the aircraft, but reportedly nothing more than just small bits and pieces were ever found. The crew went missing, although some sources quote that they had been captured by the Soviets. The cause of the accident, whether due to enemy action or structural failure, has never been fully determined.

A possible cause and the one officially released by the USAF was an oxygen system failure; the aircraft spiraled down for one hour before finally crashing in the sea. It has also been quoted that the aircraft fell victim to a SAM, but the location of the aircraft debris makes it highly unlikely that a SAM caused the loss.

Also, there were no air defense communications relating to such an action. Nevertheless, this crash caused a cessation of all missions originating from Turkey and also put an end to all missions flown over the Caspian Sea.

The end of an era

The unit continued to operate two RB-57Fs and a single TB-57C. Part of the time was spent on Project Cold Rex missions (no details known as the mission is still classified, but it may have had something to do with nuclear sampling) until 1968, when operations were suspended, due to the availability of other reconnaissance systems like satellites, and all aircraft were transferred to 58th WRS at Kirtland Air Force Base, New Mexico.

The last RB-57F left Germany on October 1, 1968, which incidentally also was the date that the squadron was inactivated. From that date onward, 58th WRS made regular deployments to Rhein-Main and continued the Cold Rex mission of 7407th SS until the mission was terminated early in 1970. The RB-57Fs, like their RB-57D predecessors, also fell victim to structural wing problems and most of them were retired to MASDC in 1972.

Thus ends one of the more colorful periods of history in the USAF. Needless to say, all of the three squadron's aircrew were unsung heroes for braving the mighty Soviet air defences, as interceptions were a very regular occurrence.

The intelligence gathered during their missions contributed to many programs, such as military readiness in Europe for all NATO Allies, strategic war planning, the development of ECM and other defensive systems, and a myriad of other operations. These units ultimately helped to end the Cold War.

Mysterious loss
RB-57F 63-13287
December 14, 1965

Map © Aviation History Research & Publishing

Aircraft known assigned to 7507th SS

Serial number	Type/model	Description/background
51-6909	Lockheed T-33A	From 4756th ADG at Moody AFB, to the 7507th in May 1956. Used by Det.1 at Bitburg. Went to the 7030th SG at Ramstein on July 9, 1959.
52-1429	Martin RB-57A	From the Wright Air Development Center delivered to the 7407th SS on August 24, 1955. Modified for Project Heart Throb. Repaired following an landing accident on November 15, 1956. Returned to USA on August 10, 1959. Reassigned to the 154th TRS (Tactical Reconnaissance Squadron) Arkansas ANG.
52-1435	Martin RB-57A	Was with the 432nd TRG at Shaw AFB. To the 7407th SS by September 1957. Modified to carry an AN/APS-60 radar. Returned to USA in June 1958 and reassigned to 2750th ABW at Wright Patterson AFB.
52-1437	Martin RB-57A	Was with the 432nd TRG at Shaw AFB. To the 7407th SS on August 8, 1957. Modified to carry an AN/APS-60 radar. Returned to USA in June 1958 and reassigned to the 2750th ABW at Wright Patterson AFB.
52-1539	Martin RB-57A	Was with the 363rd TRG at Shaw AFB. To 7407th SS on August 24, 1955. Modified for Project Heart Throb. Returned to USA on July 29, 1959, and reassigned to the 154th TRS Arkansas ANG.
52-1440	Martin RB-57A	Was with the 363rd TRG at Shaw AFB. To 7407th SS on August 24, 1955. Modified for Project Heart Throb. Returned to USA on July 29, 1959, and reassigned to the 154th TRS Arkansas ANG.
52-1442	Martin RB-57A	Was with the 363rd TRG at Shaw AFB. To 7407th SS on August 24, 1955. Modified for Project Heart Throb. Returned to USA on July 29, 1959, and reassigned to the 154th TRS Arkansas ANG.
52-1462	Martin RB-57A	Was with the 424th BS/4400 TBG at Langley AFB. To 7407th SS on August 24, 1955. Modified for Project Heart Throb. Returned to USA on July 29, 1959, and reassigned to the 154th TRS Arkansas ANG.
52-1464	Martin RB-57A	Was with the 363rd TRG at Shaw AFB. To 7407th SS on August 24, 1955. Modified for Project Heart Throb. Returned to USA on July 29, 1959, and reassigned to the 154th TRS Arkansas ANG.
52-1492	Martin RB-57A	To the 7407th SS by May 1955. Modified for Project Sharp Cut. Departed Rhein-Main on November 30, 1960 and the next few years were rather sketchy; the aircraft was removed from the USAF inventory (December 1961 -February 1965) and was likely involved in a classified project in the Far East. Nowadays, the aircraft is preserved at the Hill AFB museum.
52-1565	Martin B-57B	Was with 38th BW at Laon AB. Assigned to the 7407th SS in March 1958. Initially used for Project Hygiene but demodified at the end of 1959. It served as a trainer until departure to USA on November 7, 1960 and reassignment to the 154th TRS Arkansas ANG.
53-1545	North American RF-100A	Assigned to the 7407th SS on April 20, 1955. Transferred to the Taiwanese Air Force in December 1958.
53-1551	North American RF-100A	Assigned to the 7407th SS on May 18, 1955. Lost in an accident on October 20, 1956.
53-1554	North American RF-100A	Assigned to the 7407th SS on May 18, 1955. Transferred to the Taiwanese Air Force in December 1958.
53-3857	Martin TB-57C	From the 4080th SRW at Laughlin AFB to the 7407th SS on June 9, 1959, and remained with the unit until August 27, 1968 when it departed for reassignment to the 58th WRS at Kirtland AFB.
53-3860	Martin B-57B	Was with the 38th BW at Laon AB. Assigned to the 7407th SS in May 1958. Initially used for Project Hygiene, but it later served as a trainer until it departed for the USA on November 7, 1960, prior to reassignment to 154 TRS Arkansas ANG.
53-3963	Martin RB-57D-1	From the 4080th SRW at Laughlin AFB to the 7407th SS on June 9, 1959. Modified under the Big Safari program to Black Knight 4 standard. Back to the USA for storage on March 16, 1964.
53-3970	Martin RB-57D-2	From the 4080th SRW at Laughlin AFB to the 7407th SS on June 9, 1959. Modified under the Big Safari program to Black Knight 2 standard. To the USA on March 16, 1964. Converted to RB-57F 63-13502.
53-3972	Martin RB-57D-2	From 4025thSRS at Laughlin AF to the 7407th SS on June 9, 1959. Modified under the Big Safari program to Dinah Lee standard. Airlifted back to the USA on February 25, 1964, and stored at MASDC. Later converted to RB-57F 63-13500.
53-3974	Martin RB-57D-2	From the 4080th SRW at Laughlin AFB to the 7407th SS on June 9, 1959. Modified under the Big Safari program to Black Knight 3 standard. To the USA on March 16, 1964. Converted to RB-57F 63-13503.
53-3975	Martin RB-57D-2	From the 4080th SRW at Laughlin AFB to the 7407th SS on June 9, 1959. Modified under the Big Safari program to Black Knight 1 standard. To the USA on January 25, 1964 and converted to RB-57F 63-13501.
53-3976	Martin RB-57D-2	From the 4080th SRW at Laughlin AFB to the 7407th SS on June 9, 1959. Assigned to the 9th WRG at Andersen AFB, Guam, by 1963.
55-2711	North American F-100C	From the 36th FBW to the 7407th SS Det.1 on March 5, 1957. Assigned to the 7235th SS at Wheelus AB.
55-4264	Martin B-57E	Was with the 7235th SS at Wheelus AB. Served with 7407th SS from October 14, 1960, to mid-August 1965. Later became one of the well-known Patricia Lynn recce B-57s in Vietnam and was shot down over South Vietnam in 1968.
63-13287	Martin RB-57F	Delivered to the 7407th SS October 29, 1965. Lost over the Black Sea on December 14, 1965.
63-13500	Martin RB-57F	Delivered to the 7407th SS on April 4, 1965. To the USA on October 1, 1968, reassigned to the 58th WRS at Kirtland, AFB.
63-13502	Martin RB-57F	Delivered to the 7407th SS on February 10, 1966. Transferred to the 6021st RS at Yokota Air Base, Japan, in April 1966.
63-13503	Martin RB-57F	Delivered to the 7407th SS by April 1966. To the USA on April 4, 1968 and reassigned to the 58th WRS at Kirtland AFB.

Lineage 7407th Support Squadron
Established under 7499th Support Group in May 1955 based at Rhein-Main. Inactivated in June 30, 1974.

Secret Mission - **Index and abbreviations**

A

ABG (Air Base Group) 20, 21
ACRP (Airborne Communication Reconnaissance Program) 46
AFRES (Air Force Reserve) 46
AFS (Air Force Squadron) 8, 11, 13, 21
ALC (Air Logistics Complex) 47
AMA (Air Material Area) 20
ANG (Air National Guard) 46, 53
APN (Airborne Precision Navigation) 41
APS (Active Pulse Search) 28
ASG (Air Service Group) 21
ATRAN (Automatic Terrain Recognition And Navigation) 27, 28, 30, 34, 37, 53

B

Bases
    Aérodrome de Cerny-la Ferté-Alais, France 20
    Bitburg, Germany 19, 26, 27, 29, 37, 48, 50, 51, 52, 57
    Bodo, Norway 38, 39, 41
    Bolling, USA 35
    Brookley Field, USA 20
    Châteauroux, France 52
    Creil, France 20
    Donaldson, USA 20
    Eglin, USA 21
    Elefsis, Greece 18
    Évreux-Fauville, France 41
    Fort Worth, USA 5, 16, 19, 20, 27, 28, 34, 54
    Fürstenfeldbruck, Germany 8, 11, 12, 13, 20, 21, 50
    Fürth, Germany 11
    Giebelstadt, Germany 11, 18
    Goose Bay, Canada 48
    Groom Lake, USA 18
    Hahn, Germany 27, 37
    Hill, USA 20
    Holloman, USA 29
    Incirlik, Turkey 9, 26, 38, 39, 40, 42, 43, 45, 46
    Keflavik, Iceland 48
    Kirtland, USA 57
    Kürdemir, Azerbaijan 25
    Laon, France 30
    Leninakan/Gyumri, Armenia 42, 43
    Le Bourget, France 20
    Lechfeld, Germany 11
    NAS Port Lyauteyi, French Morocco 11
    Oberpfaffenhofen, Germany 11, 12, 21
    Osan, Japan 34
    RAF Burtonwood, England 52
    RAF Lakenheath, England 18
    RAF Leconfield, England 15
    RAF Nicosia, Cyprus 25
    RAF Upper Heyford, England 20
    Rhein-Main, Germany 5, 6, 7, 12, 28, 33, 35, 36, 37, 38, 39, 44, 46, 47, 48, 49, 52, 53, 54, 55, 56, 57
    Robins, USA 48
    Scott, USA 35
    Sembach, Germany 27, 30, 49, 53
    Sidi Slimane, Morocco 20
    Soesterberg, Netherlands 33
    Spangdahlem, Germany 23
    St. Trond/Brustem, Belgium 11
    Tempelhof, Germany 6, 12, 14, 17, 19, 32, 58
    Toul, France 23
    Tulln-Langenlebarn, Austria 15
    Wiesbaden, Germany 2, 6, 8, 11, 12, 13, 15, 16, 17, 18, 20, 21, 22, 23, 24, 25, 26, 28, 31, 32, 33, 34, 35, 36, 50, 52
        Erbenheim 13, 36
        Lucius D. Clay Kaserne 14, 36
    Yerevan, Armenia 42, 43
    Yokota, Japan 39, 41, 46, 47, 51, 57, 59
BND (Bundesnachrichtendienst) 36

C

CG (Composite Group) 21, 51
CIA (Central Intelligence Agency) 17, 18, 19, 20, 22, 24, 25, 26, 35, 52
COMINT (Communications Intelligence) 19, 26, 38, 39, 41, 42, 43, 58
CS (Composite Squadron) 10, 13, 20, 21, 23

D

DF (Direction Finding) 22, 24

E

ECM (Electronic Counter Measurement) 23, 56
ELINT (Electronic Intelligence) 8, 10, 11, 13, 15, 18, 19, 20, 21, 22, 23, 24, 26, 31, 33, 34, 35, 39, 40, 55, 58

F

FBW (Fighter Bomber Wing) 26, 52, 57
FICON (Fighter Conveyor) 37
FLIR (Forward-looking Infrared) 31

H

HBS (Headquarters and Base Service Squadron) 11, 21

I

IGN (Institute Geographic National) 10

L

LORAN (Long-range Navigation) 26
LOROP (Long-range Oblique Photography) 16

M

MASDC (Military Aircraft Storage and Disposition Center) 5, 20, 56
MTI (Moving Target Indicator) 28

N

NSA (National Security Agency) 42

O

OEL (CIA Office of ELINT) 22
Operation Vittles 24
OS (Operations Squadron) 33, 46, 47

P

PHOTINT (Photo Intelligence) 26, 58
PRG (Photo Reconnaissance Group) 11
Project/Program
    Aquatone 18
    Aunt Sue 28
    Big Safari 15, 16, 22, 27, 28
    Black Knight 1 54, 57
    Black Knight 2 57
    Black Knight 3 53, 57
    Black Knight 4 57
    Carol Ann 31
    Casey Jones 11, 20
    Cindy Fay 35
    Cold Rex 56
    Creek Grass 38, 44
    Creek Mark 46
    Creek Moose 44
    Dream Boat 38, 39, 40, 41
    Eager Beaver 35
    Flint Stone 35
    Greek Flie 35
    Half Track 28, 29, 37, 38
    Haystack 39
    Heart Throb 48, 49, 53
    Hot Pepper 20, 23, 34
    Hygiene 30, 53
    Little Guy 35
    Lulu Belle 27, 28, 29, 31, 34, 37
    Ostiary 18
    Paper Doll 54
    Pie Face 16, 17, 21, 34, 48
    Pretty Girl 20, 24
    Rivet Box 35
    Rivet Duke 33, 35
    Rivet Giant 35
    Rivet Gumbo 35
    Rivet Stem 31, 35
    Rivet Stock 22
    Sharp Cut 48, 57
    Slick Chick 48, 50, 52
    Small Fry 35
    White Christmas 54
    Wine Sap 22, 35

R

RS (Reconnaissance Squadron) 41

S

SAC (Strategic Air Command) 33
SAM (Surface-to-Air Missile) 33, 56
SG (Support Group) 8, 19, 20, 21, 27, 28, 34, 36, 57
SHORAN (Short-Range Navigation) 37
SIGINT (Signals Intelligence) 44, 55, 58
SLAR (Side-Looking Airborne Radar) 46, 53
SOC (Struck off Charge) 20, 34
SRW (Strategic Reconnaissance Wing) 5, 46, 57
SRW (Strategic Reconnasissance Wing) 45
SS (Support Squadron) 2, 3, 7, 8, 17, 19, 21, 22, 28, 33, 36, 39, 46, 48, 51, 57
SW (Strategic Wing) 34

T

TAW (Tactical Airlift Wing) 44
TDY (Temporary Duty) 45, 46, 53, 56
TRD (Terrain Reconnaissance Device) 28
TRG (Tactical Reconnaissanse Group) 57
TRS (Tactical Reconnaissance Squadron) 21, 23, 53, 57
TSCO (Top Secret Control Officer) 23

U

UHV (Ultra High Frequency) 44
USAFE (United States Air Force in Europe) 2, 6, 11, 13, 15, 18, 21, 23, 27, 28, 30, 41, 46, 49

V

V-1 Buzz Bomb 26
VHF (Very High Frequency) 44

W

WFU (Withdrawn From Use) 20